Finding the best place for

Finding the best place for prosecution

European study on jurisdiction criteria

Promoters

Prof. Dr. Tom Vander Beken
Prof. Dr. Gert Vermeulen

Researchers

Soetekin Steverlynck
Stefan Thomaes

Maklu
Antwerpen/Apeldoorn

Gert Vermeulen, Tom Vander Beken, Soetekin Steverlynck, Stefan Thomaes
Finding the best place for prosecution
Antwerpen-Apeldoorn
Maklu
2002

91 pag. - 24 x 15,5 cm
ISBN 90 6215 841 2
D/2002/1997/21
NUR 824

Maklu-Uitgevers nv
Somersstraat 13/15, 2018 Antwerpen
Koninginnelaan 96, 7315 EB Apeldoorn
info@maklu.be

Introduction

Section 1. Research Description

1. The internationalisation of crime and criminal justice has induced several problems. During the last few decades, countries have extended the application of their national criminal law to crimes which are committed outside their territory in order to prevent certain States from developing into 'safe havens' for criminals. This evolution towards more extra-territorial jurisdiction has created situations in which more than one State can claim jurisdiction.

2. Given the fact that most crimes with links in several countries are dealt with at national level by national authorities, a large number of cases are not visible at international level. And so, it is only in cases where more than one State enforces jurisdiction that concrete conflicts of jurisdiction emerge. These conflicts have significant consequences for the States and the individuals involved. Not only criminal law, but also criminal procedure law differs from country to country. The assignment of a case to a foreign country can therefore be detrimental to the offender's legal status.[1]

3. In order to contribute to the enhancement of an area of freedom, security and justice within the European Union, this paper will analyse whether the prevention or solution of jurisdiction conflicts is possible, how these matters can be arranged, and what contribution the European Union can make. The pursued goal is a realistic, short-term solution, which means that certain tracks will not be addressed.[2] Since the jurisdiction problem is inherent in all criminal justice systems, of both the common law and civil law type, the aim of the research is to create a system on a reasonable basis that is applicable to all States, with specific attention to the rights of the persons involved.

4. In this study, two parts can be distinguished: jurisdiction to prescribe and jurisdiction to enforce. This twofold structure has already been developed by T. VANDER BEKEN, *Forumverdeling in het internationaal strafrecht. De verdeling van misdrijven met aanknopingspunten in meerdere staten* (The choice of the forum in international criminal law. The division of crimes with contact points in different states).[3]

---

[1] E.g. a German sentenced in Spain is unfamiliar with the Spanish language, law and culture.

[2] Obviously the ideal solution for jurisdiction problems is the creation of a single European penal law and European penal procedure law. Nevertheless, like the establishment of a European Criminal Court, this is not a short-term solution (For further information on a European Criminal Court, see O. LAGODNY, 'Empfiehlt es sich, eine europäische Gerichtskompetenz für Strafgewaltskonflikte vorzusehen?', *Gutachten im Auftrag des Bundesministeriums der Justiz*, Berlin, März, 2001, 127-130).

[3] T. VANDER BEKEN, Forumverdeling in het internationaal strafrecht. De verdeling van misdrijven met aanknopingspunten in meerdere staten, Antwerpen-Apeldoorn, Maklu-uitgevers, 1999, 486 p.

Section 2. Methodology

5. This Grotius II-project (European Commission) was conducted from December 2001 until June 2002 by the Institute for International Research on Criminal Policy (Ghent University).

6. The study included three different phases. In first instance, a working paper was prepared to explain the causes of, and possible solutions for, jurisdiction conflicts.

7. Secondly, a meeting was organised on 22 May 2002 in Brussels (Justus Lipsius Building) to comment upon the working paper. This meeting provided the opportunity to reflect on existing proposals so that remarks could be taken into consideration for the draft of the final project findings and recommendations. The meeting started with a small gathering where, apart from the research team which consisted of Prof. Dr. TOM VANDER BEKEN, Prof. Dr. GERT VERMEULEN, STEFAN THOMAES, and SOETEKIN STEVERLYNCK, several experts were also present: Dr. M. WASMEIER and Dr. J. FRIEBERGER (European Commission), Mr. S. DE MOOR (Council of the EU), Prof. Dr. O. LAGODNY, expert in German and Austrian law (Salzburg University), Prof. Dr. J. SPENCER, expert in common law (Cambridge University), Dr. H. VAN DER WILT, expert in Dutch law (Amsterdam University), and Mr. drs. C. MULDER, expert in Nordic States law (Amsterdam University). After this meeting, the research team and the key experts attended a Eurojust meeting where the Eurojust magistrates gave their comments on the working paper. During the closing meeting, the research team and the key experts formulated several conclusions on the basis of the working paper and the Eurojust meeting.

8. Thirdly, this final report was drafted and it includes the results of the working meeting and the remarks made by W. BRUGGEMAN, deputy director of Europol. This report also contains a recommendation for a draft convention on the prevention of and solution for jurisdiction conflicts.

Section 3. Concepts

I. Jurisdiction of Crimes with Links in Different Countries

9. In the context of international criminal law, the concept of **'jurisdiction'** is used in a more restricted way than in national law, with the emphasis on the scope of these national criminal laws rather than the extent to which States exercise their right to punish. Jurisdiction may be defined as the competence of

States to determine the scope of their criminal law,[4] covering the right of a Member State to create rules of substantive criminal law with regard to certain events, the opportunity of creating procedural criminal law for that Member State's authorities to sanction infringement of these rules, and the right to apply these rules to specific cases. Jurisdiction can take different forms: the jurisdiction to prescribe (legislative competence), jurisdiction to enforce (executive competence), and jurisdiction to adjudicate (judicial competence).[5]

10. A **'link'** can be defined as

'A circumstance of the commission of a crime, giving rise to questions concerning the applicability of national law'. [6]

11. A division is made between primary jurisdiction, which is based directly on the national field of application, and derivative links, which occur when jurisdiction is derived from a competent state. This point will be developed in more detail below.

II. Kompetenz – Kompetenz

12. In contrast with the term 'link', which remains neutral regarding the concept of jurisdiction, the *Kompetenz-Kompetenz* discussion addresses the constitutive elements of the judicial claim and the determination of the extent to which States can establish judicial claims.[7] This discussion is important because of the consequences at international and individual level.

13. Three different approaches have been developed in the legal doctrine concerning the limits of the national criminal laws. The State's view on sovereignty determines which of these three views is dominant.[8]

14. A first vision, increasingly less popular, states that every State is completely free to determine the extent of its criminal law. This thesis, based on the

---

[4] G.A.M. STRIJARDS, *Internationaal strafrecht. Strafmachtsrecht*, Arnhem, Gouda Quint, 1984, Algemeen deel, 355 p.

[5] M. BOS, 'The extraterritorial jurisdiction of States', *Institute of International Law, Yearbook*, part I, 1993, 174.

[6] based on the description of 'foreign element', used by S.Z. FELLER, 'Jurisdiction over offences with a foreign element', in *A treatise on international criminal law*, M.C. BASSIOUNI, V.P. NANDA (eds.), Springfield, Illinois, Charles Thomas Publisher, 1973, Vol. II, 5.

[7] The origin of this term: BINDING or JESCHECK. for more information: A.M.M. ORIE, J.G. VAN DER MEIJS, A.M.G. SMIT, *Internationaal strafrecht*, Zwolle, Tjeenk Willink, 1991, 26; G.A.M. STRIJARDS, 1984, 113 f.f.

[8] COUNCIL OF EUROPE, EUROPEAN COMMITTEE ON CRIME PROBLEMS, Extraterritorial criminal jurisdiction, Strasbourg, Council of Europe, 1990, 26 f.f., The Council of Europe distinguishes two basic options: the judicial claim of a State is inspired either by self-protection of the State or is the expression of the solidarity between States. The former option should be approached with some caution because the State wants to protect its internal legal order while the sovereignty of other States is not taken into account.

sovereignty of States, is inspired by the fear of a 'vacuum iuris', the situation where no State can claim jurisdiction for a particular crime.[9] A current example of the decline of this theory is the Yerodia-case:[10] while the Congo stated that the jurisdiction of Belgium was excessive, Belgium replied that it was entitled to assert jurisdiction because international law does not prohibit States from exercising extraterritorial jurisdiction for war crimes and crimes against humanity, and it even permits them to do so. This judgment seems to exclude the vision that every State is completely free to determine the extent of its penal law.

15. According to a second theory, a State has only limited power to prescribe jurisdiction. Here the line is drawn by an international prohibitive regulation. As a consequence, jurisdiction cannot be claimed if it is prohibited by an international rule, and this is rarely the case.[11]

16. A final position is the converse of the latter: a State can only claim jurisdiction for crimes committed in a foreign country if an international rule explicitly provides for this.[12]

17. The Kompetenz-Kompetenz discussion also has important consequences for individuals. The question arises whether the applicability of a particular criminal law was reasonably predictable for the offender at the moment he committed the act in question. This is not the only aspect of the principle of legality that should be assured. The prohibition of retro-activity and analogous interpretation, for example, also have to be considered.

Part I. Jurisdiction to prescribe

Introduction

18. The aim of this part of the study is to give an overview of the different contact points which States use to prescribe jurisdiction, starting from a distinction between primary jurisdiction and derivative jurisdiction.

19. At the moment, it is sometimes more difficult to find a State which has no jurisdiction than to find one that has jurisdiction. Indeed, many States believe that they must prescribe jurisdiction not only for offences which have been committed on their own territory, but also for crimes committed outside their

---

[9] S.Z. FELLER, Concurrent criminal jurisdiction in the international sphere, *Israel law review*, 1981, 41.

[10] INTERNATIONAL COURT OF JUSTICE, case concerning the arrest warrant of 11 April 2000, Democratic Republic of the Congo v. Belgium, 14 February 2002, N° 121.

[11] E.g. the Lotus-case (PERMANENT COURT OF INTERNATIONAL JUSTICE, The Hague, 7 September 1927, *Revue Internationale de Droit Pénal*, 1927, 326-362), explained further below.

[12] A.M.M. ORIE, J.G. VAN DER MEIJS and A.M.G. SMIT, 1991, 27.

territory in order to avoid situations in which nothing can be done against unwanted behaviour and to prevent certain States from becoming 'safe havens' for criminals.[13] As a result, conflicts of jurisdiction are inevitable because too many States are in a position to start prosecution. The European Union seems to stimulate this trend, since the first priority set forth in many legal papers is that Member States prescribe jurisdiction.[14]

Section 1. Primary Jurisdiction

I. Territorial Jurisdiction

20. The *territoriality principle* is accepted everywhere as the first and most important contact point and the authority of a State to prescribe jurisdiction over acts that take place on its own territory is uncontested.[15]

21. There would seem to be no conflicts of jurisdiction if all States prescribe jurisdiction only on the basis of their own national territory. This is, of course, a rather simplified reflection of reality, as in practice it is not always easy to determine where an offence has been committed. This determination is important and depends on the criminal-political appreciation by a State (cf. several localisation theories).[16] The prosecution of certain computer-related crimes is a good example of a situation where it is really difficult to determine the location where the offence has been committed because cyberspace has no boundaries.

22. States are, to a large extent, free to make a choice between a broad localisation theory and a more restricted localisation theory, as this decision

---

[13] For general considerations of extra-territorial jurisdiction: F.A. MANN, 'The international doctrine of jurisdiction in international law', *Collected Courese of the Hague Academy of International Law*, 1964, 9-162; F.A. MANN, 'The doctrine of international jurisdiction revisited after twenty years', *Collected Courese of the Hague Academy of International Law*, 1984, 11-115; I. BROWNLIE, *Principles of public international law*, Oxford, Clarendon Press, 1990, 298 f.f., O. SCHACHTER, *International law in theory and practice*, Dordrecht-Boston-London, Martinus Nijhoff Publishers, 1991, 253-270, M. BOS, 'The extra-territorrial jurisdiction of states', *Institute of International law, Yearbook*, 1993, part I, 13-190, and R. JENNINGS and A. WATTS, *Oppenheim's international law*, London-New-York, 1996, volume I.Peace, 456 f.f.

[14] COMMISSION OF THE EUROPEAN COMMUNITIES, Mutual Recognition of Decisions in Criminal Matters among the EU Member States and Jurisdiction, Discussion Paper with questions for experts, 2001, 11.

[15] COUNCIL OF EUROPE, EUROPEAN COMMITTEE ON CRIME PROBLEMS, Extraterritorial criminal jurisdiction, Strasbourg, Council of Europe, 1990, 8. Within the Corpus juris, this is not under discussion since it starts with the notion of a European territory. There the approach of one single jurisdictional unit for crimes against the European Community is to be preferred over the approach of achieving better co-ordination between 15 territories that are considered as separate judicial units, see Corpus Juris 2000, Florence, May 1999, *ERA- forum* 3, 2001, 59.

[16] G.A.M. STRIJARDS, 1984, 225; M.-C. FAYARD, 'La localisation internationale de l'infraction', *Revue de Science Criminelle et de Droit Pénal Comparé*, 1968, 753-779; S.Z. FELLER, 1973, II, 19-25; A.M.M. ORIE, J.G. VAN DER MEIJS and A.M.G. SMIT, 1991, 35-36.

cannot be justified on the basis of legal arguments, but forms part of the criminal politics of a country.[17] The broad theory gives rise to a quasi-unlimited opportunity to enforce jurisdiction, while the more restricted theory reduces the opportunities of enforcing jurisdiction on the basis of the territory of the State. Countries that choose a broad localisation theory do not take into account the fact that certain crimes can also be prosecuted in other States on the basis of the same principle and give rise to many conflicts of jurisdiction.

23. In practice, it is possible that several States consider themselves competent to start prosecution on the basis of the territoriality principle.[18] In civil law countries, as well as in common law countries, the concept of territory is broadly interpreted.[19] A possible solution for conflicts could consequently be the application of a more restricted definition of the concept of 'territory'.

II. Extraterritorial Jurisdiction

24. Besides the 'locus delicti', States can also apply one of the principles of extraterritorial jurisdiction to start prosecution. In other words: States can prescribe jurisdiction for offences which cannot be located on their own territory. This form of prosecution is mostly subsidiary to the 'locus delicti'. States can prescribe extraterritorial jurisdiction if the offender is one of their nationals (active personality principle, statute of perpetrator)[20] and also in situations where certain acts are committed against their nationals (passive personality principle, statute of victim).[21] In addition, States can also start prosecution on the basis of the protection principle and the universality principle.

25. In practice, most States only prescribe jurisdiction on the basis of the *active personality principle* [22] if the State where the offence has been committed does

---

[17] T. VANDER BEKEN, 1999, 42.

[18] An example: State A wants to enforce territorial jurisdiction because the consequences of the criminal offence can be localised on their territory and State B considers itself to be in a better position to start prosecution as the perpetrator was 'active' on its territory.

[19] T. VANDER BEKEN, 1999, 43-47 and 73.

[20] Or when he is one of their officials, permanent residents, or even a legal person based on its territory

[21] COMMISSION OF THE EUROPEAN COMMUNITIES, Mutual Recognition of Decisions in Criminal Matters among the EU Member States and Jurisdiction, Discussion Paper with questions for experts, 2001, 10.

[22] A distinction can be made between three different interpretations of this principle: the *absolute* application with the nationality of the perpetrator as the first and most important contact point to prescribe jurisdiction, the *unlimited* application with the territory as most important contact point, but with the facility also to prescribe jurisdiction on the basis of the nationality of the offender, and, finally, a *limited* application where a State only prescribes jurisdiction if the State where the offence has been committed does not prosecute, and with the presence of the suspect on the territory and double incrimination as requirements (D. OEHLER, *Internationales Strafrecht. Geltungsbereich des Strafrechts. Internationales Rechtshilferecht. Recht der Gemeinschaften, Völkerstrafrecht*, Köln-Berlin-Bonn-München, Carl Heymanns Verlag KG, 1983, 444-448 and H. DONNEDIEU DE VARBES, *Les principes modernes du droit pénal international*, Sirey, Paris, 1928, 69-76).

not prosecute or is unable to start prosecution.[23] Under international law, the admissibility of the limited active personality principle is not debated (in contrast with the unlimited application of this principle), because there is hardly any interference with the internal matters of another State and there is a requirement of double incrimination which is important for the legal status of the suspect.[24] States sometimes impose additional conditions on the applicability of this principle (e.g. presence of the offender, official notification by the State in which the offence has been committed, or an instruction to prosecute from the Minister of Justice).[25]

26. States can also prescribe jurisdiction on the basis of the *passive personality principle*, inspired by the idea that a State must protect its own nationals, even when they are abroad. Although this reasoning seems acceptable, in practice there is great resistance to it. OEHLER, for example, considers this principle *'das schlechteste aller Prinzipien'*,[26] as it could create a lot of conflicts of jurisdiction. States sometimes apply this principle because they have misgivings about the legal system of the State where a crime has been committed against one of their nationals. In some States the principle of passive personality is applicable to all offences, in others only to serious ones. There is an international trend towards the inclusion of provisions in treaties encouraging the Contracting States to prescribe jurisdiction on the basis of the passive personality principle.[27] Art. 9 of the Proposal for a Council Framework Decision on combating terrorism is a good example of this trend.[28]

27. States also assume the right to prescribe jurisdiction for crimes committed outside their territory, but with the intention of damaging their national interests. The main justification for this *protection principle* is that the protection of these fundamental interests cannot be left to other States or that other States do not consider that such interests require the protection of the criminal law. In some countries, it is applicable to an extremely limited number of offences, in other countries to a very large number of crimes.[29] Jurisdiction conflicts are possible, as the principle of protection is a powerful contact point (the requirement of double incrimination or other prosecution conditions are not imposed). The protection principle could also affect fundamental human rights (e.g. freedom of speech) and the legal status of victims and perpetrators because prosecution could completely surprise them. A lot of States make use of the protection

---

[23] T. VANDER BEKEN, 1999, 106-108.

[24] D. OEHLER, 1983, 445; H. DONNEDIEU DE VARBES, 1928, 59-65.

[25] COUNCIL OF EUROPE, EUROPEAN COMMITTEE ON CRIME PROBLEMS, Extraterritorial criminal jurisdiction, Strasbourg, Council of Europe, 1990, 11.

[26] D. OEHLER, 1983, 116.

[27] COUNCIL OF EUROPE, EUROPEAN COMMITTEE ON CRIME PROBLEMS, Extraterritorial criminal jurisdiction, Strasbourg, Council of Europe, 1990, 12.

[28] *'Each Member State shall take the necessary measures to establish its jurisdiction over the offences referred to in art. 1 to 3 where the offence has been committed against the institutions or people of the Member State in question or against an institution of the European Union or a body set up in accordance with the Treaties establishing the European Communities and the Treaty on European Union and based in that Member State'* (COUNCIL OF THE EUROPAN UNION, proposal for a Council Framework Decision on combating terrorism, Brussels, 7 december 2001, 11).

[29] COUNCIL OF EUROPE, EUROPEAN COMMITTEE ON CRIME PROBLEMS, Extraterritorial criminal jurisdiction, Strasbourg, Council of Europe, 1990, 13.

principle to combat international criminality on the basis that all States should be in a position to prosecute all crimes and to avoid impunity. Another tendency is that some countries stretch the concept of 'fundamental interests' to include other interests (e.g. the capital market, certain industrial interests,…).[30] This evolution is very detrimental to the development of a distribution mechanism for offences with contact points in several States.[31]

28. Moreover, States can start prosecution for very serious offences where the perpetrator is considered to be a danger to the world (*hostis generis humani*), although there is no direct contact point with the crime. They can therefore prescribe jurisdiction on the basis of the *universality principle* without taking into account the 'locus delicti', the offenders or the victims.[32] Specialist literature in this field often refers to the *Barcelona Traction case*,[33] where the International Court of Justice referred to an *erga omnes* obligation for the whole international community:

> *'By their very nature [they] [...] are the concern of all States. In view of the importance of the rights involved, all States can be held to have a legal interest in their protection, they are obligations erga omnes.'* [34]

29. The list of crimes with universal jurisdiction is limited and must find a basis in international law. However, there is no consensus as to which crimes the universality principle could be applied to. There is no doubt that war crimes and crimes against peace and mankind (cf. Conventions of Geneva), counterfeiting, criminal offences against international protected people, and terrorism appear on this list.[35] It is possible to make a distinction between two different groups of countries: States which have the intention to limit the application of the universality principle (e.g. The Netherlands) because it gives rise to conflicts of jurisdiction, and States which believe in a broad application of this principle (e.g. France, Germany and England).[36] Countries whose concern is an international 'proper administration of justice' have to limit the application of the universality principle to avoid conflicts of jurisdiction.

---

[30] COUNCIL OF EUROPE, EUROPEAN COMMITTEE ON CRIME PROBLEMS, Extraterritorial criminal jurisdiction, Strasbourg, Council of Europe, 1990, 14.
[31] T. VANDER BEKEN, 1999, 152-153.
[32] M.R. MOK en R.A.A. DIJK, 'Toepassing van het Nederlands strafrecht op buiten Nederland begane delicten', *Handelingen 1980 der Nederlandse Juristen-Vereniging deel 1, tweede stuk*, 1980, 146-147; D. OEHLER, 1983, 538; H. DONNEDIEU DE VARBES, 1928, 135; T. MERON, 'International criminalization of internal atrocities', *American Journal of International Law*, 1995, 554; J.J. PAUST, M.C. BASSIOUNI, S. WILLIAMS, M. SCHARF, J. GURULLÉ and B. ZAGARIS, *International Criminal Law. Cases and Materials*, Durham – North Carolina, Carolina Academic Press, 1996, 95; O. SCHACHTER, *International Law in theory and practice*, Dordrecht – Boston – Londen, Martinus Nijhoff Publishers, 1991, 267; R. HIGGINS, *Problems and process. International law and how we use it*, Oxford, Clarendon Press, 1994, 56-57.
[33] J.J. PAUST, M.C. BASSIOUNI, S. WILLIAMS, M. SCHARF, J. GURULLÉ and B. ZAGARIS 1996, 95.
[34] 5 February 1970, *(Case Concerning the Barcelona Traction, Light and Power Company Limited)*, *International Court of Justice Reports*, 1970, 3, par. 33.
[35] T. VANDER BEKEN, 1999, 154-156.
[36] T. VANDER BEKEN, 1999, 178-180.

Section 2. Derivative Jurisdiction

30. The aforementioned principles are based on contact points that are considered to be strong enough to allow States to prescribe and to enforce jurisdiction unilaterally. However, sometimes it is possible to prescribe jurisdiction in situations where the criminal offence has no direct contact point with the State or where the State only has a contact point that is too minor to justify jurisdiction. In these cases, the State can enforce jurisdiction, derived from a State that has one of the recognised contact points with the crime. Derivative jurisdiction can only be enforced in substitution of a State that has original jurisdiction.[37] It is possible to make a distinction between two variants of derivative jurisdiction: *substitution* and *adoption of proceedings*. It is not easy to make this distinction because this matter is situated on the dividing line between jurisdiction and mutual legal assistance.

31. Substitution is based on the *aut dedere aut iudicare* principle and is inextricably linked with extradition. On the basis of this concept, a State decides to start prosecution in situations where they do not extradite a foreigner. The concept of substitution stems from the idea that criminals cannot remain unpunished. The distinction between substitution and application of the universality principle is difficult to make because both notions are used interchangeably, although they are fundamentally different. The difference between substitution and the universality principle is that it is only possible to prosecute if other States do not start prosecution themselves. Substitution is, in theory, possible for all forms of offences, since there is no requirement that the crimes have to be very serious.

32. At first sight, there are some similarities with the active personality principle, since the main function of this principle is to make prosecution possible if the State where the crime has been committed (or another State) does not start prosecution. Substitution has the same purpose.[38] In other words, it is possible to consider both concepts as complementary. States that apply the active personality principle enforce jurisdiction on the basis of the nationality of the perpetrator. Such a strong contact point is absent in situations of substitution, because the State can only enforce jurisdiction deduced from another State.[39]

33. Substitution could be problematic for suspects and victims of criminal offences, since prosecution could come as a complete surprise to them, although there are some guarantees (e.g. the requirement of double incrimination). The suspect may be tried in a country by which he did not expect prosecution at the moment he has committed the crimes. Jurisdiction on the basis of substitution

---

[37] T. VANDER BEKEN, 1999, 183.
[38] C. PAPPAS, *Stellvertretende Strafrechtsplege. Zugleich ein Beitrag zur Ausdehnung deutscher Strafgewalt nach § 7 Abs. 2 Nr. 2 StGB*, Freiburg im Breisgau, Max-Planck-Institut für ausländisches und internationales Strafrecht, 1996, 16.
[39] C. PAPPAS, 1996, 19-20; D. OEHLER, 1983, 507.

could also create confusion for the victim because his case could be dealt with in an 'unknown' State.[40]

34. Adoption of proceedings is a form of derivative jurisdiction dependent on a specific request by a State that has original jurisdiction. In specialist literature, the concepts of *transfer of proceedings* and *adoption of proceedings* are used interchangeably . Although both notions are the expression of one interaction between States, it is useful to make a distinction between them . This part of the research deals with the concept of adoption of proceedings as a variant of derivative jurisdiction. In the research of BAAIJENS-VAN GELOVEN,[41] adoption of proceedings is subdivided into three different parts:

- there is a request to start prosecution;
- this request comes from a State that is in a position to prosecute;
- prosecution in the requested State takes places or continues on the grounds of this request.

35. 'Proper administration of justice' is the justification of the system of adoption of proceedings. In these cases, a State enforces jurisdiction not because it can justify a strong contact point, but because it is in the best position to do this.[42] States cannot unilaterally divide jurisdiction on the grounds of proper administration of justice because this principle alone is too weak. Consequently, jurisdiction on the basis of proper administration of justice can only be enforced at the explicit request of a State with original jurisdiction. The onus is on the State that considers that another State is in a better position to take over prosecution, and not on the State that ultimately will enforce jurisdiction.

36. The scope for the State that takes over jurisdiction must be restricted because the adoption of proceedings could surprise the suspects and victims concerned completely and could therefore affect their legal status. At the moment, the determination of the place of the trial is a barely predictable policy decision for both, instead of a clear matter of criminal law and criminal procedure.[43]

37. There are two options to justify the predictability of the instrument of adoption of proceedings and to avoid *forum shopping*.[44] PAPPAS believes that a foregoing determination (in a treaty) of general criteria of proper administration of justice is sufficient to cope with the requirements of predictability and certainty. However, according to her, it is not necessary that the parties concerned can determine, in advance, the judge who will try their case.[45] The

[40] T. VANDER BEKEN, 1999, 192; C. PAPPAS, 1996, 183-188.
[41] Y.G.M. BAAIJENS-VAN GELOVEN, *Overdracht en overname van strafvervolging*, Arnhem, Gouda Quint, 1996, 29.
[42] A.H.J. SWART, 'De overdracht van strafvervolgingen', *Nederlands Juristenblad*, 1982, 211; A.H.J. SWART, *Goede rechtsbedeling en internationale rechtshulp in strafzaken*, Deventer, Kluwer, 1983, 3; A.H.J. SWART, 'Internationalisering van de strafrechtspleging', in C. KELK a.o. (eds.), *Grenzen en mogelijkheden. Opstellen over en rondom de strafrechtspleging*, Nijmegen, Ars Aequi Libri, 1984, 117.
[43] D. OEHLER, 1983, 434-435.
[44] T. VANDER BEKEN, 1999, 214; O. LAGODNY, 2001, 70-72.
[45] C. PAPPAS, 1996, 137.

second option is to involve the suspect and the victim more closely in this procedure, since proper administration of justice is too vague and weak as a contact point for jurisdiction. Suspects and victims must be treated as persons with a place and a voice and must therefore have a decisive influence on this transfer and adoption procedure to justify prosecution.[46] The second option seems more consistent in substance. [47]

38. The instrument of adoption of proceedings is, in practice, not attractive for States as it creates more work and it is based on solidarity. Furthermore, the result is that people are prosecuted, although the State does not wish, or is not able, to prosecute on its own initiative because there is no real contact point.

Section 3. Conclusion

39. Presently, too many States are in a position to prescribe jurisdiction so that conflicts of jurisdiction are inevitable (e.g. one State applies the territoriality principle and another applies one of the personality principles). Although this problem can partly be avoided if States restrict their claims for jurisdiction, a large number of conflicts will be left unsolved since overlaps of jurisdiction are still possible. A system of exclusive territorial jurisdiction seems to be an option that is not feasible, as this requires a fundamental political change.

40. It is worth mentioning that in 1976 the Benelux countries, which resemble each other in different fields, have made an endeavour to restrict their jurisdiction, defining the criteria which supply jurisdiction.[48] This draft tried to avoid abstract conflicts of jurisdiction by describing the links on which jurisdiction can be based. Although the draft has never developed into a convention and the text is not spectacular because of the general rules, its starting point is clear: in the interests of both international co-operation and the individuals, jurisdiction should be prescribed in moderation.

41. The trend towards more jurisdiction is contrary to the aim of Art 31.d TEU, according to which the EU wants to prevent conflicts of jurisdiction. A good example of this trend is Art. 7 of the Council framework Decision of 29 May 2000 on increasing protection by criminal penalties and other sanctions against

---

[46] G. VERMEULEN, T. VANDER BEKEN, P. ZANDERS, B. DE RUYVER, *Internationale samenwerking in strafzaken en rechtsbescherming*, Brussel, Politeia, 194; N. WITSCHI,, *Die Übernahme der Strafverfolgung nach künftigen schweizerischem Recht*, Bern, Verlag Stämpfli, 1977, 83; A.H.J. SWART, 1982, 222-223; A.H.J. SWART, 1983, 16.
[47] T. VANDER BEKEN, 1999, 215.
[48] R. SCREVENS, 'Collaboration en matière pénale et tentatives d'harmonisation du droit pénal dans certains groupes d'états', *Droit pénal européen, Europees Strafrecht, European Criminal Law*, Brussel, Presses Universitaires de Bruxelles, 1970, 612-616; B. DE SCHUTTER, 'Samenwerking in strafzaken en pogingen tot harmonisatie van het strafrecht in de Beneluxlanden', *Droit pénal européen, Europees Strafrecht, European criminal law*, Brussel, Presses Universitaires de Bruxelles, 1970, 590-593.

counterfeiting in connection with the introduction of the Euro.[49] The European Union should therefore consider changing its policy with regard to jurisdiction. Instead of stimulating Member States to prescribe jurisdiction, it might be recommended that the EU gives a clear message to the States to temper their jurisdiction policy. This recommendation could prevent a number of jurisdiction conflicts in the future.

Part II. Jurisdiction to enforce

Introduction

42. The previous section has analysed the opportunities of prescribing jurisdiction, stressing the importance of limiting the extension of jurisdiction, which has been a trend within the EU during the last decades. A thorough study of this subject leads to the conclusion that this restraint on prescribing jurisdiction in itself is not satisfactory. The division of jurisdiction of crimes implies much more: States can also decide not to prosecute even though they are competent, since the division implies both the attraction and the repulsion of cases.

43. In this context, two extreme situations may occur: it is possible that there are too many prosecutions for a certain case,[50] or that there is a situation of inertia, caused by a lack of claims. This behaviour occurs mostly when the interests of another State or the international community are jeopardised, instead of the national interests of a State.[51] Consequently, the problem of prosecution of crimes with links in different countries is not caused by a shortage of opportunities to exercise jurisdiction, but by the way in which States enforce jurisdiction.

44. In the sections above, the importance of Art. 31 TEU has been emphasised in the context of the avoidance of abstract conflicts of jurisdiction. In this section , this article is also relevant for the evasion of concrete conflicts of jurisdiction.

---

[49] Each Member State shall take the necessary measures to establish its jurisdiction over the offences referred to in Articles 3 to 5, where the offence is committed in whole or in part within its territory (Council framework Decision of 29 May 2000 on increasing protection by criminal penalties and other sanctions against counterfeiting in connection with the introduction of the Euro, *O.J.*, 14.6.2000, L 140,1).

[50] E.g. the Lockerbie-case: two Libyans caused the explosion of an American aeroplane by a bomb above Lockerbie in Scotland. This led to a conflict between the three countries, all claiming jurisdiction. Another example is the situation where the international 'ne bis in idem' principle is not respected, as in the Dost-cases in Germany, A.M.M. ORIE, 'Internationale strafrechtelijke aspecten van de Dost-affaire', *Nederlands Juristenblad*, 1976, 1045-1059.

[51] E.g. the Pinochet case, where collective responsibility led to inertia until Belgium requested his extradition, see C. INGELSE and H. VAN DER WILT, De zaak Pinochet. Over universele rechtsmacht en Hollandse benepenheid, *NJB* (Ned.) 1996, 280-285.

45. Currently, a concrete conflict of jurisdiction is solved by (a) unilateral action of the States, resulting in pushing the conflict to extremes and the persistency of the prosecution by several States, or (b) deliberation or compliance with the international 'ne bis in idem' principle. Since the first option is not to be supported in the European area of freedom, security and justice and is not to be recommended, we will focus our analyses on the amicable solution of conflicts by deliberation and respect for the 'ne bis in idem' principle.

46. The following section will examine to what extent States feel restricted from prosecuting because of the 'ne bis in idem' principle, in a situation where there is a definitive decision, and the principle of proper administration of justice when this is not the case. This twofold division is meant to give a clear overview, but it should be borne in mind that the international 'ne bis in idem' principle is obviously an essential element for the proper administration of justice in itself.

Section 1. The International Ne Bis In Idem Principle

47. Several initiatives to introduce an international 'ne bis in idem' principle have been taken by different institutions, some more fruitful than others.[52] In addition to the international treaties which recognise the international ne bis in idem principle explicitly, various conventions on mutual legal assistance[53] also contain this principle, although they relate to the aspects of mutual legal assistance instead of giving it general recognition . A study of these treaties shows that this principle is widely recognised on an international level. Even if the universal 'ne bis in idem' principle is not yet generally accepted, it is clear that important progress has already been made.[54]

48. Still, the existence of several gaps of the international 'ne bis in idem' principle give rise to additional jurisdiction problems. Because of the shortage of ratification and the opportunity to implement exceptions[55] to the principle, the 'ne bis in idem' rule sometimes defeats its own object. Furthermore, on the basis of the international texts, it is difficult to determine what exactly constitutes an "idem".[56]

49. The most substantial criticism of the existing 'ne bis' principle is its narrow application within the EU. Paragraph 54 of the Schengen Implementing

---

[52] Art. 50 of the Charter of Fundamental Rights of the European Union, *OJ*, C 364 of 18 December 2000; Art. 54-58 Convention of 19 June 1990 applying the Schengen Agreement; Art. 1 Convention of 25 May 1987 between the Member States of the European Communities on double jeopardy; Benelux Conventions of 26 September 1968 and 11 May 1974; ...

[53] E.g. Art. 9 of the European Convention on extradition of 13 December 1957; Art. 6 e and 11 of the European Convention on the international validity of criminal judgments of 28 May 1970; ...

[54] O. LAGODNY, 2001, 61.

[55] E.g. Art. 2 of the EPC Convention on double jeopardy of 25 May 1987.

[56] C. VAN DEN WYNGAERT, *The transformations of international criminal law as a response to the challenge of organised crime*, Antwerp, Universitaire Instelling Antwerpen, 1998, 37-39.

Convention[57] is only relevant to final decisions, although it seems more appropriate to expand the concept to other decisions, such as the decision not to prosecute, the decision to provide immunity of prosecution, alternative settlement, and dismissal.

50. The idea of a broader 'ne bis in idem' principle should be correlated to mutual legal assistance since the 'ne bis' principle currently provides no absolute grounds for refusal of mutual legal assistance. It is contradictory to prohibit a second prosecution for facts that have already been judged, but at the same time to allow mutual legal assistance, such as extradition, concerning that offender. In order to avoid co-operation between States that can lead to an infraction of this principle, mutual legal assistance is to be put on the same level as decisions.[58]

51. This goes hand in hand with the regrettable absence of a European criminal record database,[59] which will be examined below, since, for the moment, it is hardly possible for a State to be aware of the fact that there has been a decision concerning a certain case in another State.[60]

Section 2. Proper Administration of Justice

Introduction

52. Action should be taken to avoid concrete conflicts of jurisdiction by restraining the exercise of jurisdiction. This limitation can be established in two different ways, whereby the exercise of jurisdiction is dependent on the proper administration of justice. The first possibility is to build in a hierarchy in the claims of jurisdiction so that it can be decided by virtue of a treaty which State is in the best position to prosecute. The second view starts with the idea that it is impossible to structure these claims hierarchically because the decision should be examined case by case. The following section will investigate both views.

---

[57] Convention of 19 June 1990 applying the Schengen Agreement of 14 June 1985 between the Governments of the States of the Benelux Economic Union, the Federal Republic of Germany and the French Republic, on the gradual abolition of checks at their common borders, URL: ue.eu.int/ejn/data/vol_c/9_autres_textes/schengen/indexen.html.
[58] G. VERMEULEN, *Wederzijdse rechtshulp in strafzaken in de Europese Unie: naar een volwaardige rechtshulpruimte voor de Lidstaten?,* Antwerpen-Apeldoorn, Maklu, 1999, 97; G. VERMEULEN, T. VANDER BEKEN, E. DE BUSSER, C. VAN DEN WYNGAERT, G. STESSENS, A. MASSET AND C. MEUNIER, *Een nieuwe Belgische wetgeving inzake internationale rechtshulp in strafzaken,* Antwerpen – Apeldoorn, Maklu, 2002, 108.
[59] COMMISSION OF THE EUROPEAN COMMUNITIES, Communication from the Commission to the Council and the European Parliament on the Mutual Recognition of Final Decisions in Criminal Matters, Brussels, 26/07/2000, COM(2000) 495 final, 7.
[60] JUSTICE, EU co-operation in criminal matters, response to specific proposals, February 2001, 13, URL: www.justice.org.uk/publications/listofpublications/index.html; H. XANTHAKI, *The use of criminal records as a means of preventing organised crime in the areas of money laundering and public procurement: the need for Europe-wide collaboration*, Falcone Project JHA/1999/FAL/197, Sir William Dale Centre for Legislative Studies, London, vol. 1, 99 p.

53. It should be emphasised that the search for solutions in this context is not new. In the past, several efforts have already been made to solve the problem of jurisdiction. Although the attempts to set up a hierarchical list were not very fruitful, they are worth mentioning because of their contribution to the thinking process.

I. A Hierarchical List of Jurisdiction Criteria

A. Underlying Ideas

54. Since the Second World War, the emphasis has shifted significantly. New accents in the division problem have been inspired by the special attention for the delinquent and his resocialisation.[61] Secondly, the trend of expanding jurisdiction has continued, catalysed by the fight against terrorism.[62] The idea has arisen that such sorts of criminality could not remain unpunished and should be prosecuted if no extradition is requested (*aut dedere, aut judicare*).[63]

55. This concern for resocialisation and avoiding impunity was the breeding ground for the rise of a new approach to conflicts of jurisdiction. This view focused on avoiding the *conversion* of abstract conflicts into concrete conflicts,[64] instead of the *evasion* of abstract conflicts.

56. From the eighties onwards, this resocialisation idea has been moderated. As a consequence, the concept of proper administration of justice is not principally focused on attention for the suspect and the best place of prosecution, but can be applied in the most diverse ways. This complicates the division problem, since the answers on the 'best' place of prosecution are equally valuable if certain minimum requirements are fulfilled.

---

[61] M. ANCEL, *La défence sociale nouvelle. Un mouvement de politique criminelle humaniste*, Parijs, Cujas, 1954, 183 p.; M; ANCEL, *La défence sociale*, Parijs, Presses Universitaires de France, 1989, 127 p., B. DE RUYVER, *De strafrechtelijke politiek gevoerd onder de socialistische Ministers van Justitie, E. Vandervelde, P. Vermeylen en A. Vranckx*, Antwerpen-Arnhem, Kluwer-Gouda Quint, 1988, 182.
[62] J.J. LAMBERT, *Terrorims and hostages in international law. A commentary on the Hostages Convention 1979, Cambridge*, Grotius Publications, 1990, 28-57; L.S. SUNGA, *The emerging system of international criminal law. Developments of codification and implementation*. Den Haag-London-Boston, Kluwer law International, 1997, 191-205; B. DE SCHUTTER, 'Problems of jurisdiction in the international control of repression of terrorism', in *International terrorism and political crimes*, M.C. BASSIOUNI (ed.), Springfield, Illinois, Charles Thomas Publisher, 1975, 377-390.
[63] C. VAN DEN WYNGAERT, *The political offence exception to extradition. The delicate problem of balancing the rights of the individual and the international public order*, Boston-Antwerpen-London-Frankfurt, Kluwer, 1980, 218-229.
[64] Concretised e.g. by the transfer of proceedings.

B. Different Attempts

57. Inspired by the concern to reduce the positive conflicts of jurisdiction by collectively limiting their claims to jurisdiction, the Convention of Montevideo of 23 January 1889 between South American States is worth mentioning.[65]

58. During the sixties, the Council of Europe also made an effort along the same line, starting with Recommendation 420 (1965) and the Draft Convention concerning international conflicts of jurisdiction. The aim of this attempt was to create a hierarchical list based on the proper administration of justice in order to avoid concrete, positive conflicts of jurisdiction. Three arguments supported the setting up of a convention, and these were :

> 1. International law recognises the existence of different forms of jurisdiction, so the exclusion of positive conflicts of jurisdiction is impossible;
>
> 2. Even jurisdiction based on territoriality can cause conflicts if States use various localisation criteria;
>
> 3. Such conflicts are undesirable, since it can lead to a situation where an offender is tried several times in different countries.

59. Furthermore, a hierarchical list was set up, making a distinction between primary and secondary claims to jurisdiction. The State where the crime has been committed and the State claiming jurisdiction on the basis of the protection principle were positioned on top, followed by claims based on the active personality principle and the universality principle.[66]

60. After the submission of the Draft Convention to the Committee of Ministers, a Subcommittee of the European Committee on Crime Problems was charged with the further redaction of the Draft Convention. This Subcommittee obviously had a divergent view on the problem. It did not support the idea of a hierarchy of criteria since this was perceived as being too rigid and mechanical to adjust to concrete situations. Additionally, the Subcommittee did not agree that the place where the crime was committed is always the most appropriate forum of jurisdiction. Inspired by the resocialisation idea, the decision has been made that the place of prosecution was not to be appointed beforehand, since specific elements proper to every case should be taken into consideration.[67]

---

[65] Treaty on International Penal Law, Montevideo, 23 January 1889, amended by the Convention of Montevideo of 19 March 1940; The contracting States were Argentinia, Bolivia, Paraguay, Peru and Uruguay, *Supplement to the American Jounal of International Law*, 1935, 638-639; D. OEHLER, 1983, 13.

[66] Explanatory Report on the European Convention on the Transfer of Proceedings in Criminal Matters, 1972, in E. MÜLLER-RAPPARD and M.C. BASSIOUNI, European inter-state co-operation in criminal matters, 1991, *E.T.S.* n°73, 16; F. THOMAS, *De Europese rechtshulpverdragen in strafzaken. Ontstaan en evolutie van een Europees strafrechtsbeleid van uitlevering tot overdracht van strafvervolging,* Gent, Story Scientia, 1980, 34.

[67] These documents are not available anymore, for the content see T. VANDER BEKEN, 1999, 384-393, O. LAGODNY, 2001, 47-52.

61. Nevertheless, the use of such a list was not innovative. After all, provisions in this sense have already been included in the NAVO-Status Convention of 1951[68] and afterwards, for example, in the BASS-Convention of 1969[69] and the Draft International Criminal Code of 1980[70].

62. Finally the original Draft Convention had little remains, so the idea of a hierarchy of jurisdiction criteria has been replaced by the transfer of proceedings. The explanatory report of the European Convention of Transfer of Proceedings in Criminal Matters (1972) gives a clear view of the discussion:

> *'The assumption that it is normally most appropriate to prosecute an offence where it has been committed is not justified. Rehabilitation of the offender which is increasingly given weight in modern penal law requires that the sanction be imposed and enforced where the reformative aim can be most successfully pursued, that is normally in the State in which the offender has family or social ties or will take up residence after the enforcement of the sanction.*
>
> *On the other hand it is clear that difficulties in securing evidence will often be a consideration militating against the transmission of proceedings from the State where the offence has been committed to another State. The weight to be given in each case to conflicting considerations cannot be decided by completely general rules. The decision must be taken in the light of particular facts of each case. By attempting in this way to arrive at an agreement between the various States concerned, it will be possible to avoid the difficulties which they would encounter by a prior acceptance of a system restricting their power to impose sanctions'.*[71]

63. It is clear that the efforts to set up a list of criteria were not very fruitful, since such a hierarchical solution seemed too inflexible and mechanical to be suitable for any concrete situation. A list of criteria is consequently still considered as unfeasible and undesirable.

---

[68] Art. VII.3 of the Agreement between the Parties to the North Atlantic Treaty regarding the status of their forces, 19 June 1951 in G. VERMEULEN and T. VANDER BEKEN, *Compendium Internationaal Strafrecht*, IA, 19/06/51, 1-19, URL: www.nato.int/docu/basictxt/b510619a.htm; O. LAGODNY, 2001, 97-98.

[69] Art 10 Convention 29 avril 1969 concernant la coopération administrative et judiciaire dans le domaine des réglementations se rapportant à la réalisation des objectifs de l'Union économique Benelux, La Haye, *Moniteur Belge*, 17 february 1971.

[70] Art. V.1.1 Draft International Criminal Code in M.C. BASSIOUNI, *A draft international criminal code and draft statute for an international criminal tribunal*, Dordrecht, Boston, Lancaster, Martinus Nijhoff Publishers, 1987, 191.

[71] Explanatory Report on the European Convention on the Transfer of Proceedings in Criminal Matters, 1972, in E. MÜLLER-RAPPARD and M.C. BASSIOUNI, European inter-state co-operation in criminal matters, 1991, *E.T.S.* n°73, 23.

II. Reasonable Enforcement of Jurisdiction

Introduction

64. Since a hierarchical list of criteria is not suitable, deliberation seems to be a more efficient solution to deal with situations where several States claim jurisdiction and to prevent conflicts of jurisdiction. In the European Commission discussion paper for experts, deliberation is defined as:

> *'trying, on an ad-hoc basis, possibly using non-binding guidelines, to reach consensus on which of the Member States interested should go ahead with proceedings in situations where the jurisdiction of two or more Member States is given'.*[72]

65. In the context of deliberation, it is important to draw attention to the subsidiarity principle, which means that not every case with contact points in more than one State can be deliberated at a European level, such as, for example, a Belgian who commits shoplifting in the Netherlands. Such a case falls into the hands of a national prosecutor and will probably never reach the discussion at an international level.

66. In addition, attention should be paid to the possibility of splitting up and merging certain cases, specifically in the framework of joint investigations. The question whether it is preferable to concentrate the committals for trial in a single Member State or to assign different components of a complex case to various countries, and the problem which country should consequently be competent for the prosecution, should be answered on an identical base as other crimes with links in various countries. Deliberation will obviously play an important role, based on the proper administration of justice.

67. This chapter starts with an analysis of the applicable criteria on which a judgment should be based. Furthermore, attention will be paid to several organisational requirements, making a distinction between the two different stages of the proceedings where deliberation can take place: (I) the pre-trial phase and (II) the trial phase. Finally, (III) the post-trial phase handles the possibility of a higher court to review the enforced jurisdiction.

68. A European Criminal Court is not an option at the moment, as the competence to judge on all cases where more than one State can enforce jurisdiction would provide this court with an enormous caseload. Furthermore, attention will be paid to the information that should be used to support the deliberation, and to what extent the outcome of this consultation procedure should be binding on the Member States.

---

[72] COMMISSION OF THE EUROPEAN COMMUNITIES, Mutual Recognition of Decisions in Criminal Matters among the EU Member States and Jurisdiction, Discussion Paper with questions for experts, 2001, 5.

A. Reasonableness as a Guiding Principle

69. This section intends to set out the criteria on which the deliberation is to be based in order to attain a proper administration of justice, as mentioned above .

70. It is important to stress that the concept of proper administration of justice does not necessarily imply swift and effective law enforcement. A balance is required between the necessity of prosecution and humanitarian considerations such as resocialisation of the accused, prosecution in a country where the accused is familiar with the law and the language, the interests of the victim etc.[73] Proper administration also covers considerations of criminal procedure (e.g. prevention of double prosecution, avoidance of sentence by default,...).

71. Two sorts of criteria can be distinguished, one set being positive and the other negative. Positive criteria of any kind are mentioned in various international treaties and judgments such as the European Convention on the International Validity of Criminal Judgments (1970),[74] the European Convention on the Transfer of Proceedings in Criminal Matters (1972),[75] the Protocol amending the Treaty on extradition between the Government of Canada and the Government of the United States of America (1971),[76] the cases United States of America v. Cotroni and United States of America v. El Zein,[77] etc ... .

72. For example, Art. 8 of the European Convention on the Transfer of Proceedings in Criminal Matters[78] indicates the cases in which one contracting State may request taking proceedings in another contracting State.[79] A request is possible if:

1. *the suspected person is ordinarily resident in the requested State;*
2. *the suspected person is a national of the requested State or if that State is his State of origin;*
3. *the suspected person is undergoing or is to undergo a sentence involving deprivation of liberty in its territory;*

---

[73] C. VAN DEN WYNGAERT, Corpus Juris, Parquet européen et juge national vers une chambre préliminaire européenne, *Agon,* august 1999, N°23, 3.
[74] Art. 5 European Convention on the International Validity of Criminal Judgments, 28 May 1970, *E.T.S.*, n° 70.
[75] Art. 8 European Convention on the Transfer of Proceedings in Criminal Matters, 15 May 1972, *E.T.S.*, n° 73; Explanatory Report on the European Convention on the Transfer of Proceedings in Criminal Matters, 1972, in E. MÜLLER-RAPPARD and M.C. BASSIOUNI, European inter-state cooperation in criminal matters, 1991, *E.T.S.* n°73, 37.
[76] Protocol amending the Treaty on extradition between the Government of Canada and the Government of the United States of America, Washington, 3 December 1971, URL: www2.lexum.umontreal.ca/ca_us/en/cts.1991.37.en.cfm?langue=en.
[77] United States of America v. El Zein, URL: www.lexum.umontreal.ca/csc-scc/en/pub/1989/vol1/html/1989scr1_1469.html.
[78] European Convention on the Transfer of proceedings in criminal matters, 15 May 1972, *E.T.S.*, n° 70.
[79] O. LAGODNY divides the criteria of Article 8 into three different groups: *Resozialisierung, Prozessökonomie* and *Vermeindung von Abwesenheitsurteilen* (O. LAGODNY, 2001, 83).

4. *proceedings for the same or other offences are being taken against the suspected person by its prosecuting authorities;*
5. *the most important items of evidence are located in its territory;*
6. *the enforcement in its territory of a possible future sentence is likely to improve the prospects for the social rehabilitation of the person sentenced;*
7. *unlike in the requesting State, the presence of the suspected person can be ensured at the hearing of proceedings in its territory or*
8. *unlike the requesting State, it could enforce a possible future sentence.*

73. These criteria are used in several other texts and are based on Art. 5 of the Convention on the International Validity of Criminal Judgments. They are linked with Art. 11 of the European Convention on the Transfer of Proceedings in Criminal Matters (1972), which indicates the cases where the requested State is allowed to refuse the request. The conditions are not cumulative and the list is exhaustive.

74. The first four of the above-mentioned criteria are objective, while the last four involve a subjective appreciation by the requesting State. These rules are clearly to the detriment of the offender. It should be stressed that these criteria are not listed in order of importance and none has overriding importance for the aims of the Convention.[80]

75. The Corpus Juris, which will be examined further below, has also devoted an Article to the forum choice.[81] The criteria of Art. 26 § 2 seem one dimensional, given the continuous returning and primordial necessity to strike a balance between the interests of the State and those of the persons involved. It seems to see the State's interest as decisive:

> *'Each case is judged in the Member State which seems appropriate in the interests of efficient administration of justice, any conflict of jurisdiction being settled according to the rules set out hereafter (art. 28). The principal criteria for the choice are the following:*
> *1.the State where the greater part of evidence is found;*
> *2.the State of residence or of nationality of the accused (or the principal persons accused);*
> *3.the State where the economic impact of the offence is the greatest.'*

76. Other critical remarks are the observation that the criteria laid down in Art. 26 § 2 are not sufficiently precise and that the functioning is not clear. In addition, whilst some criteria are well known to most Member States, others are less well known and not widely accepted in national systems, for example the 'evidence criteria' (German, Austrian, Spanish and Luxembourg reports).[82]

---

[80] Explanatory Report on the European Convention on the Transfer of Proceedings in Criminal Matters, 1972, in E. MÜLLER-RAPPARD and M.C. BASSIOUNI, European inter-state co-operation in criminal matters, 1991, *E.T.S.* n°73, 37.

[81] M. DELMAS-MARTY and J.A.E. VERVAELE, *The implementation of the Corpus Juris in the Member States*, Vol I, Antwerpen-Groningen-Oxford, Intersentia, 2000, 206-207.

[82] M. DELMAS-MARTY and J.A.E. VERVAELE, 2000, 345.

77. No pre-established hierarchy of criteria appears in Art. 26, and this was a deliberate choice by the editors of the Corpus Juris.

> *'It did not seem desirable to impose an order of priority between the different criteria (...). That choice is to be made by the EPP, under the eventual control of the ECJ (...) in order to maintain maximum flexibility.'*

78. However, some authors state that, in relation to certain national legal systems, such flexibility seems incompatible with the need to guarantee the rights of the citizens, who must know where they will be judged. According to them, the principle of the 'national legal judge', which has constitutional status in some countries and which can also be derived from the jurisprudence of the European Court of Human Rights, constitutes the main objection to the present wording of Art. 26. However, such a system would be preferred over the risks of excessive rigidity associated with a system with a hierarchy of principles.[83]

79. Another example can be drawn from the Rome Statute of the International Criminal Court (ICC).[84] According to Art. 17.1 of this Statute on the admissibility of cases[85], the ICC is complementary to the national courts and dependent on their collaboration.[86] The second paragraph of this Article states that in order to determine unwillingness in a particular case, the ICC will consider, having regard to the principles of due process recognised by international law, whether one or more of the following exist, as appropriate:

(a) The proceedings were, or are, being undertaken or the national decision was made for the purpose of shielding the person concerned from criminal responsibility for crimes within the jurisdiction of the Court referred to in Article 5;

(b) There has been an unjustified delay in the proceedings which, in the circumstances, is inconsistent with an intent to bring the person concerned to justice;

(c) The proceedings were not, or are not, being conducted independently or impartially, and they were, or are, being conducted in a manner which,

---

[83] M. DELMAS-MARTY and J.A.E. VERVAELE, 2000, 345-346; W. VAN GERVEN, 'Constitutional conditions for a Public Prosecutor's Office at the European level' in G. DE KERCHOVE and A. WEYEMBERGH (ed.), *Vers un espace judiciaire pénal européen*, Bruxelles, Institut d'études européennes, 2000, 323.

[84] Rome Statute of the International Criminal Court, 17 July 1998, URL, www.un.org/law/icc/statute/romefra.htm.

[85] A case is inadmissible if (a) the case is being investigated or prosecuted by a State which has jurisdiction over it, if (b) the case has been investigated by a State which has jurisdiction over it and the State has decided not to prosecute the person concerned, if (c) the person concerned has already been tried for conduct which is the subject of the complaint or if (d) the case is not of sufficient gravity to justify further action by the Court.

[86] T. VANDER BEKEN, 'De moeilijke zoektocht naar het beste forum voor internationale misdrijven. De ad hoc tribunalen als ideale oplossing?', WOUTERS, J. and PANKEN, H. (eds.), *De Genocidewet in internationaal perspectief*, Gent, Larcier, 2002, 84.

in the circumstances, is inconsistent with an intent to bring the person concerned to justice.

80. The option of the *ad hoc* Tribunals, where the international court has priority over the national courts, is not used in this research.[87]

81. The European Convention on the Transfer of Proceedings and the Corpus Juris are examples of a list of positive criteria. Nevertheless, it seems more fruitful to focus on the negative criteria and consequently prohibit jurisdiction based on impermissible criteria. This could be the case e.g. if the criterion of the harshest punishment is decisive.

82. In the above-mentioned judgments United States of America v. Cotroni and United States of America v. El Zein, the factors affecting the choice of whether or not to prosecute in a country contain positive and negative criteria:

- where was the impact of the offence felt or likely to be have been felt;
- which jurisdiction has the greater interest in prosecuting the offence;
- which police force played the major role in the development of the case;
- which jurisdiction has laid charges;
- which jurisdiction has the most comprehensive case;
- which jurisdiction is ready to proceed with the trial;
- where is the evidence located;
- whether the evidence is mobile;
- the number of accused involved and whether they can be gathered together in one place for trial;
- in what jurisdiction were most of the acts in furtherance of the crime committed;
- the nationality and residence of the accused; and
- the severity of the sentence the accused is likely to receive in each jurisdiction.

83. It is striking that both positive and negative criteria are combined without any distinction in this list, and this makes it difficult to conceptualise. The analysis of both the positive and negative criteria leads to the view that the traditional criteria are necessary for the exercise of jurisdiction, but not sufficient. An additional requirement could be the reasonableness *in concreto* of the exercise of jurisdiction. This additional criterion has first been developed in 1965 and again in 1986 by the American Law Institute.[88]

---

[87] For information on the ad hoc tribunals see: T. VANDER BEKEN, 'De moeilijke zoektocht naar het beste forum voor internationale misdrijven. De ad hoc tribunalen als ideale oplossing?', WOUTERS, J. and PANKEN, H. (eds.), 2002, 75-94.

[88] AMERICAN LAW INSTITUTE, art. 40 Restatement (Second) of the Foreign Relations Law of the United States, 1965 and § 402, 403 Restatement (Third) of the Foreign Relations of Law of the United States, 1986. The former Restatement is only a comity-recommendation, while the latter is obligatory and can consequently be compelled before a judge.

84. Art. 40 of the Restatement of 1965 prescribes:

'Where two States have jurisdiction to prescribe and enforce rules of law and the rules they may prescribe require inconsistent conduct upon the part of a person, each State is required by international law to consider, in good faith, moderating the exercise of its enforcement jurisdiction, in the light of such factors as:
> *1.vital national interests of each of the States;*
> *2.the extent and the nature of the hardship that inconsistent enforcement actions would impose upon the person;*
> *3.the extent to which the required conduct is to take place in the territory of the other State;*
> *4.the nationality of the person and*
> *5.the extent to which enforcement by action of either State can reasonably be expected to achieve compliance with the rule prescribed by that State'*

85. The Restatement of 1986 has the same subject, but differs in the sense that it formulates an explicit prohibition to exercise jurisdiction if this seems unreasonable in the light of the criteria mentioned. § 402 confirms the legitimacy of jurisdiction on the basis of the traditional links. § 403 adds that the presence of these links is not sufficient since the criterion of reasonableness is not taken into account. To reach this goal, § 403 adds an explicit interdiction to exercise jurisdiction on the basis of § 402 if this has unreasonable consequences:

'(1)Even when one of the bases for jurisdiction under § 402 is present, a State may not exercise jurisdiction to prescribe law with respect to a person or activity having connections with another State when the exercise of jurisdiction is unreasonable.
(2)Whether exercise of jurisdiction over a person or activity is unreasonable is determined by evaluating all relevant factors, including, where appropriate:
a. the link of the activity to the territory of the regulating State, i.e. the extent to which the activity takes place within the territory, or has substantial, direct, and foreseeable effect upon or in the territory;
b. the connections, such as nationality, residence, or economic activity, between the regulating State and the person principally responsible for the activity to be regulated, or between that State and those whom the regulation is designed to protect;
c. the character of the activity to be regulated, the importance of regulation to the regulating State, the extent to which other States regulate such activity, and the degree to which the desirability of such regulation is generally accepted;
d. the existence of justified expectations that might be protected or hurt by the regulation;
e. the importance of the regulation to the international, political, legal or economic system;
f. the extent to which the regulation is consistent with the traditions of the international system;
g. the extent to which another State may have an interest in regulating the activity and
h. the likelihood of conflict with regulation by another State.

(3)When more than one State has reasonable basis for exercising jurisdiction over a person or activity, but the prescriptions by two or more States are in conflict, each State has an obligation to evaluate its own as well as the other States' interest in exercising jurisdiction in light of all the relevant factors, including those set out in subsection (2) and should defer to the other States if that State's interest in clearly greater.'

86. The idea of reasonable enforcement of jurisdiction is compatible with the existing 'abuse of process' in common law,[89] and the German 'Abwägungsfehlerlehre'.[90] Since the reasonableness criterion is also closely connected to the concept of proper administration of justice, the question arises whether the latter should also grant subjective rights to individuals. The criterion of reasonableness has, after all, developed in the Restatements from a rule of conduct towards a right which can be compelled.[91] It seems appropriate to create a non-hierarchical list of potentially reasonable criteria in order to enhance the transparency of EU legislation.[92] This list could contain the principle of territoriality, Art. 8 of the European Convention on Transfer of Proceedings and victim oriented criteria. The completion of negative criteria could be left to competent prosecutorial bodies including Eurojust (infra), by means of a praetorian development. These could be used as prosecution guidelines, enhancing transparency by their public character. A thorough motivation, which mentions the applied criteria, seems essential, no matter which body decides on the forum choice.

---

[89] The principle of abuse of process is premised on the notion that a court is not behaving in a legitimate manner unless it discharges its public duty of protecting the innocent from wrongful conviction and of protecting the moral integrity of the criminal process, while at the same time keeping in mind the public interest in the conviction of the guilty (A. L.-T. CHOO, *Abuse of process and judicial stays of criminal proceedings*, Oxford, Clarendon Press, 1993, 182).

[90] This concept is used in German law regarding the use of criminal evidence. It states that evidence may not be used if there is an imbalance between the interests of the prosecution and the interests of the citizens. See W. BEULKE, *Strafprozessrecht*, Heidelberg, C.F. Müller Verlag, 2000, 224-225 and, using the term '*normative Fehlerfolgenlehre*' K. ROGALL, 'Grundsatzfragen der Beweisverbote' in *Beweisverbote in Ländern der EU und vergleichbaren Rechtsordnungen / Exclusion of Evidence Within the EU and Beyond*, F. HÖPFEL and B. HUBER (eds.), Freiburg im Breisgau, Max-Planck-Institut für ausländisches und internationals Strafrecht, 1999, 119-148 (139-140); O. LAGODNY, 2001, 117.

[91] F.L. MORRISON, *German Yearbook of international law*, 1986, 423; AMERICAN LAW INSTITUTE, 1986, 246 and 254; W. WENGLER, 'Völkerrechtliche Schranken der Beeinflussung auslandverknüpften Verhaltens durch Massnahmen des Staatlichen Rechts' in *German Yearbook of International Law*, 1988, 449-450; X., 'Constructing the state extraterritorially: jurisdictional discourse, the national interest and transnational norms', *Harvard Law Review*, 1990, 1274 and 1278.

[92] The Green Paper on criminal-law protection of the financial interests of the Community and the establishment of a European Prosecutor also expresses the Commission's preference for the combination of the criteria as a set of concordant rules, rather than being ranked on a hierarchical basis, COMMISSION OF THE EUROPEAN COMMUNITIES, Green Paper on criminal-law protection of the financial interests of the Community and the establishment of a European Prosecutor, Brussels, 11/12/2001, COM(2001) 715 final, 53, URL: europa.eu.int/comm/anti_fraud/livre_vert.

B. Organisational Requirements

1. Pre-trial Phase

a. Deliberation between States

87. Legal authorities sometimes communicate with colleagues in other countries concerning cases where more than one State is in a position to prosecute. Through this way of consultation, possible jurisdiction conflicts can be prevented.

88. Most of the existing legal texts only aim at obliging Member States to prescribe jurisdiction, without paying attention to the practical consequences. However, several EU instruments already foresee a consultation procedure.[93] A good example of such a procedure is Art. 7.3 of the Council Framework decision of 29 May 2000 on increasing protection by criminal penalties and other sanctions against counterfeiting in connection with the introduction of the Euro.[94]

89. In the Council of Europe Convention of 15 May 1972 on the transfer of proceedings in criminal matters, a consultation procedure is also stipulated. Article 30 of this Convention states that any Contracting State which is aware of proceedings pending in another Contracting State against the same person in respect of the same offence must consider whether it can either waive or suspend its own proceedings, or transfer them to the other State. The other State must be informed if it is not possible to waive or to suspend proceedings in good time and before judgment is given on the merits. In this eventuality, the States concerned must try to determine which of them shall continue to conduct proceedings on the basis of Article 8. This Article has been addressed above.[95]

90. This consultation procedure seems to be a very good instrument to solve conflicts of competence. Therefore, it is regrettable that only five EU Member States (Austria, Denmark, Netherlands, Spain, and Sweden) have ratified this Convention. This is even more so, as this Convention pays attention to the legal status of the victim and the offender involved.

---

[93] COMMISSION OF THE EUROPEAN COMMUNITIES, Mutual Recognition of Decisions in Criminal Matters among the EU Member States and Jurisdiction, Discussion Paper with questions for experts, 2001, 11.

[94] Where more than one Member State has jurisdiction and has the opportunity for viable prosecution of an offence based on the same facts, the Member States involved shall co-operate in deciding which Member State shall prosecute the offender or offenders with a view to centralising the prosecution in a single Member State, where possible (Council Framework Decision of 29 May 2000 on increasing protection by criminal penalties and other sanctions against counterfeiting in connection with the introduction of the Euro, *O.J.*, 14.6.2000, L 140,1).

[95] O. LAGODNY, 2001, 84.

91. The instruments transfer and adoption of proceedings first of all guarantee that proceedings cannot be taken in the requested State unless the offence in respect of which the proceedings are requested would also be an offence if committed in its territory and unless, in these circumstances, the offender could also be sanctioned under its own law.[96] In Article 8 of the Convention on the transfer of proceedings in criminal matters several forum selection criteria are included based on humanitarian motives, such as the resocialisation of the convicted person. It is striking that the position of the victim is not considered to be a valuable starting point for the inter-state transfer of proceedings or enforcement, although the legal position of the victim could be seriously affected by the forum selection process.[97]

92. Article 17 provides the suspect with the opportunity to present his views on the matter before the State makes a decision on the request. It seems appropriate that victims should also be given the chance to give their views on the case, in order to protect the interests of the defence.[98] Other guarantees for the suspect are the 'ne bis in idem' principle (Art. 35), an opportunity to appeal against the decision of the Minister of Justice and the lex mitior principle.[99]

93. The Netherlands has had an extensive law on transfer of proceedings since 6 March 1985. A right of veto[100] was not included in this law, although several discussions were held in relation to this matter.[101] A criminal judge sometimes has the opportunity to review the decision to transfer. In the Netherlands, the suspected person has the opportunity to challenge the transfer to the court after he has been informed of the transfer. The victim can also oppose to the transfer. A transfer is then only possible after authorisation by the judge. In the law of 1985, the content of the concept of proper administration of justice was rather restricted. This was changed by a Minister of Justice circular,[102] through which this concept was alligned with the ratio legis of Art. 8.[103] The regulation in the Netherlands is fairly detailed and forms a counter-weight for forum shopping.

94. The Nordic States (Denmark, Finland, Iceland, Norway, and Sweden) also have a consultation mechanism, based on trust, which is comparable to the procedure laid down in the Council of Europe Convention on the Transfer of

---

[96] Art. 7.1. of the European Convention on the Transfer of Proceedings in Criminal Matters
[97] G. VERMEULEN, 1999, 244-245.
[98] G. VERMEULEN, T. VANDER BEKEN, E. DE BUSSER, C. VAN DEN WYNGAERT, G. STESSENS, A. MASSET AND C. MEUNIER, 2002, 229.
[99] In the requested State, the sanction applicable to the offence shall be that prescribed by its own law unless that law provides otherwise. Where the competence of the requested State is exclusively grounded on Art. 2, the sanction pronounced in that State shall not be more severe than that provided for in the law of the requesting State (Art. 25).
[100] It is interesting to mention that a right of veto for the victim (Art. 1.2) was foreseen in a Benelux Convention of 11 May 1974 on transfer of proceedings. However, this convention never came into force.
[101] T. VANDER BEKEN, 1999, 297-298.
[102] Circulaire van de Minister van Justitie aan het college van procureurs-generaal inzake de overdracht en overname van strafvervolging, *Nederlandse Staatscourant*, 27 juli 2001, nr. 143.
[103] G. VERMEULEN, T. VANDER BEKEN, E. DE BUSSER, C. VAN DEN WYNGAERT, G. STESSENS, A. MASSET AND C. MEUNIER, 2002, 211.

Proceedings (1972).[104] This co-operation between the Nordic prosecution services is based on a co-operation agreement concluded by the Nordic supreme prosecutors on 6 February 1970, and amended on 12 October 1972. In the Evaluation Report on Finland on Mutual Legal Assistance and Urgent Requests for the Tracing and Restraint of property, reference is made to this agreement:

> *'This agreement regulates prosecution in a different Nordic Country than where the offence was committed. In addition, the long tradition of cooperation in law drafting has led to the fact that the Nordic Countries have nationally brought into force similar legislation, which enables flexible and efficient administration of justice in criminal matters between the Countries.'* [105]

95. The public prosecutor of the Nordic State where the offence has been committed takes the initiative for the transfer of proceedings and contacts a public prosecutor in another Nordic country. A decision is made, taking account of the rules of evidence[106] and the position of the victim. The public prosecutors of the Nordic States compare the pros and cons of the transfer. However, certain aspects cannot be taken into consideration. [107]

96. Most transfers concern cases where no victim is involved. However, if victims are involved in a case, they have a strong voice in the transfer procedure. A distinction can be made between ordinary cases and more complicated cases. In the latter, the office of the Nordic supreme prosecutors intervenes if the public prosecutors cannot come to a settlement. Exceptionally, the Nordic supreme prosecutors must try to find a solution themselves. An example of such a situation is the *Scandinavian Star Incident*.[108]

97. An intervention of a European body is favourable, as deliberation between States is not institutionalised and does not automatically lead to a solution that can be compelled. European bodies should handle crimes with links in several countries that cannot be dealt with on a national level. In the following chapter, the option of a European Public Prosecutor and Eurojust will both be discussed.

---

[104] European Convention on the Transfer of Proceedings in Criminal Matters, 15 May 1972, *E.T.S.*, n° 73.

[105] COUNCIL OF THE EUROPEAN UNION, evaluation report on Finland on Mutual Legal Assistance and Urgent Requests for the Tracing and Restraint of property, Brussels, 7 July 2000, 43 p., URL: ue.eu.int/ejn/data/evaluation/09392.en.pdf.

[106] A transfer is more probable when a suspect makes a full confession.

[107] Good examples are a more severe sanction in the other Nordic State, and the use of 'criminal tricks' (e.g. a situation where a telephone tap is not possible in the requesting State contrary to the requested State).

[108] On 6 April 1990 the ferry 'Scandinavian Star' left Oslo (Norway), under the command of Captain Hugo Larsen, bound for Frederikshavn (Denmark). Several hours later a fire broke out that was to claim the lives of 158 people on board. Most passengers came from Norway, some from Denmark, and a few from Sweden. The day after, the ship was taken under tow to a small town in Sweden. Following the tragedy, Sweden, Denmark, and Norway agreed to set up a committee of inquiry to investigate the reasons for the tragedy. The fire was started deliberately. However, no one has been charged with starting the fire. Norway wanted to prosecute the ferry company, but had no legal basis in its legislation to prosecute. Denmark had this opportunity, so an agreement between Denmark and Norway was necessary to transfer proceedings, URL: www.fire.org.uk/marine/papers/scanstar.htm.

b. Intervention of a European Body

b.1. European Public Prosecutor

b.1.1. General

98. The Corpus Juris[109], set up for the protection of the financial interests of the European Union, seems to give an adequate framework in terms of competence of jurisdiction. In order to conduct investigations for these specific kinds of crime, a European Public Prosecutor is proposed (EPP), comprising a Director of European Public Prosecutions (EDPP) and European Delegated Public Prosecutors (EdelPPs).[110] A judge of freedoms, being a national magistrate, would take the judicial control of the pre-trial investigations for his or her account. Co-operation with Olaf and Europol will be ensured.[111]

99. The vital question whether the EPP would have the power or the duty to proceed has been examined extensively in the Green Paper on criminal law protection of the financial interests of the Community and the establishment of a European Prosecutor.[112] The Commission's preference is expressed for a mandatory prosecution system, modified by certain exceptions. He would have the power to close a case not only on technical grounds that he cannot escape, but also on discretionary grounds. By these means, an exception on the mandatory prosecution principle might be made on the basis of the potential impact of the potential impact of the proceedings on the outcome of the case, the importance of the case for the protection of the Community's financial interests, or the effectiveness of recovery of the sums corresponding to the financial interests that are violated.

100. These proposals, which are not yet in force, are based on Art. 280 of the EC Treaty as amended by the Treaty of Amsterdam, stating that appropriate measures should be taken to protect the financial interests of the Community.[113]

101. The PFI instruments,[114] which are the common base for the criminal law protection of the Union's financial interests, have not yet entered into force since

---

[109] M. DELMAS-MARTY, *Corpus Juris, portant dispositions pénales pour la protection des intérêts financiers de l'Union européenne,* Antwerpen-Groningen-Oxford, Intersentia Rechtswetenschappen, 1998, 189 p.

[110] M. DELMAS-MARTY, J.A.E. VERVAELE, *The implementation of the Corpus Juris in the Member States volume IV,* Antwerpen-Groningen-Oxford, Intersentia, 2001, 530 p.

[111] COMITE DE SURVEILLANCE DE L'OLAF, 'Avis 2/2002 sur le livre vert sur la protection pénale des intérêts financiers communautaires et la création du procureur européen', *Agon,* N° 34, 2002, 5.

[112] COMMISSION OF THE EUROPEAN COMMUNITIES, Green Paper on criminal-law protection of the financial interests of the Community and the establishment of a European Prosecutor, Brussels, 11/12/2001, COM(2001) 715 final, 44, URL: europa.eu.int/comm/anti_fraud/livre_vert.

[113] COMMISSION OF THE EUROPEAN COMMUNITIES, Proposal for a Directive of the European Parliament and of the Council on the criminal-law protection of the Community's financial interests, Brussels, 23/05/2001, COM(2001) 272 final.

they still lack the ratification of all the Member States. A Directive on the criminal law protection of the Community's financial interests has been proposed.[115]

b.1.2. Competence

102. The criteria[116] adopted by the Member States in the context of the third pillar aim to ensure that there is at least one Member State that has jurisdiction. This does not necessarily mean that a *single* Member State has jurisdiction. If there are contact points in several States, it seems most appropriate that the European Prosecutor would determine the Member State in which the case is to be committed for trial. In this context, he should be able to decide to concentrate the committals for trial in a single Member State and also to sever the prosecution so as to send different components of a complex case for trial in as many different Member States as may be necessary. In any event, the choice of a national court at the preparatory stage should not predetermine the Member State of trial.[117]

103. The allocation of jurisdiction to one Member State may have certain implications with regard to Member States' international obligations since these may contain agreements concerning the establishment of jurisdiction for certain cases that are contradictory to the decision of the European Prosecutor.[118] On the other hand, this decision has several advantages. First of all, it will be much easier for the other Member States to recognise and therefore accept that State's sentence compared to a situation whereby its own authorities would also have been competent to decide. Forum shopping, by either the prosecution or the defence, could be prevented. Furthermore, there would be less of a risk of 'ne bis in idem' situations arising.

104. As regards the review of the choice of a Member State for trial by the EPP, two possible options have been suggested. The first one, based on trust in all the national legal systems, is to leave him wholly responsible for the choice. This can be to the detriment of the offender if the court is selected on an unfair basis, since the EPP would in this case have absolute discretionary power. A second option is to entrust the review function to the double supervision of the judge of

---

[114] These are the instruments for the protection of the Community's financial interests, being The Convention on the protection of the European Community's financial interests of 26 July 1995, *O.J.*, C313, 23/10/1996; First Protocol of 27 September 1996, *O.J.*, C313, 23/10/1996; Protocol of 29 November 1996 on the interpretation of the PFI Convention and its Protocols by the Court of Justice, *O.J.*, C 151, 20/05/1997; Second Protocol of 19 June 1997, *O.J.*, C 221, 19/07/1997.

[115] EUROPEAN PARLIAMENT, Draft opinion on the proposal for a directive on the criminal-law protection of the Community's financial interests, 12/10/2001, 2001/0115(COD).

[116] Art. 4 of the Convention of 25/07/1995 and Art. 6 of the Protocol of 27/09/1996.

[117] COMMISSION OF THE EUROPEAN COMMUNITIES, Green Paper on criminal-law protection of the financial interests of the Community and the establishment of a European Prosecutor, Brussels, 11/12/2001, COM(2001) 715 final, 52-53, URL: europa.eu.int/comm/anti_fraud/livre_vert.

[118] COMMISSION OF THE EUROPEAN UNION, Communication of the commission to the Council on mutual recognition of final decisions in criminal matters, Brussels 26/07/2000, COM(2000) 495.

freedoms and the national court. The question arises whether the review of legality by reference to national law should be extended to manifest errors in the choice of Member State. Even without giving the national court the power to rule against the EPP's discretionary choice of forum, review of abuse or manifest error entails the possibility that one or more Member States might decline the case. Theoretically, the jurisdiction criteria of the PFI Convention of 25 July 1995, mentioned above, should eliminate this kind of situation, but in practice this option does suggest that there could be a few cases of declined jurisdiction and possibly even of negative conflicts of jurisdiction.[119]

b.1.3. European Preliminary Chamber

105. The idea has been launched to entrust the control of the EPP to a European preliminary chamber at the moment of the closing of the preliminary investigation in order to avoid an a posteriori control.[120] Its creation was to be proposed at the European Council in Laeken in the light of the proposed Art. 225a [121] of the Treaty of the European Union, which would allow the Council to create judicial panels to hear and determine certain cases at first instance.[122]

106. The starting point is the idea that the national judge of freedoms is fundamentally disabled in his function to control the EPP because, necessarily, he is merely able to base a decision on the part of the case submitted to him.

107. The idea of this preliminary chamber has been introduced because of several shortcomings in the original proposition. First of all, the national judge of freedoms will often have to deal with a part of the procedure that has taken place in a foreign country. Consequently the hypothesis that this judge has to apply foreign law in addition to his own law and the Corpus Juris is not unreal. A second disadvantage is that forum shopping is possible by the EPP on the hypothesis that several judges of freedoms were caught.[123]

108. This chamber could be composed of judges from the European Court of Justice or could be a newly established organ which receives the prejudicial questions of the national judge of freedoms. Whether these questions can be raised by the EPP or a citizen is not clear. Although the option of a preliminary chamber seems feasible, it is no longer mentioned in the Green Paper.

---

[119] COMMISSION OF THE EUROPEAN COMMUNITIES, Green Paper on criminal-law protection of the financial interests of the Community and the establishment of a European Prosecutor, Brussels, 11/12/2001, COM(2001) 715 final, 53-54, URL: europa.eu.int/comm/anti_fraud/livre_vert.

[120] C. VAN DEN WYNGAERT, 'Corpus Juris, parquet européen et juge national vers une chambre préliminaire européenne', *Agon,* 1999, N° 23, 6.

[121] Draft Treaty Articles 280 and 280a, URL: www.euroscep.dircon.co.uk/corpus8.htm#Top. The proposed text amendments to Treaty Article 280 failed to receive agreement from Member States during the Nice Summit.

[122] ERA, *ERA-forum* 3, Study on 'penal and administrative sanctions, settlement, whistleblowing and Corpus Juris in the candidate countries', 2001, 53.

[123] G. STESSENS, 'Het Corpus Juris in een stroomversnelling, het Europees openbaar ministerie in aantocht?', *Panopticon* 2000, 274.

b.1.4. Conclusion

109. In the Corpus Juris project, the EPP has decision-making power. This project has the theoretical advantage that it is problem solving, as the decision of the EPP can be compelled. However, there seem to be more disadvantages. First of all, the Corpus Juris project is a rather immature concept based on a fictive European territory. Furthermore, it is only set up for the protection of the financial interests of the European Union. Finally, the Corpus Juris functions top-down and intervenes too strongly in the positive injunction power of the Member States.

b.2. Eurojust

b.2.1. General

110. The proposal to set up Eurojust was submitted to the Heads of State and Government by the Ministers for Justice at the informal meeting of Ministers for Justice and Home Affairs held in Finland on the 16th and the 17th of September 1999.[124] The reason for setting up Eurojust was that international police co-operation in Western Europe had expanded so quickly over the past two decades that judicial co-operation could not keep pace. The police had, for example, been entrusted with more autonomy to exchange and communicate information without prior judicial permission. The Schengen Implementing Convention[125] and the Europol Convention[126] embodied this evolution in the field of intra-European police information exchange. The fact that the police had growing power to share information within the EU was normally not so much a problem provided that the necessary data protection rules were observed. More problematic was, and still is, the shift towards more independent and proactive operational policing.[127]

111. In most systems, operational policing and evidence gathering are to be supervised and directed by prosecuting or investigating magistrates or officials in order to avoid problematic situations.[128] The IRT case in the Netherlands, which eventually led to the installation of the so-called Van Traa Committee on

---

[124] COUNCIL OF THE EUROPEAN UNION, Exploratory thoughts concerning Eurojust, Brussels, 4 February 2000, 2.
[125] Convention of 19 June 1990 applying the Schengen Agreement of 14 June 1985 between the Governments of the States of the Benelux Economic Union, the Federal Republic of Germany and the French Republic, on the gradual abolition of checks at their common borders, URL: ue.eu.int/ejn/data/vol_c/9_autres_textes/ schengen/indexen.html.
[126] Convention of 26 July 1995 on the establishment of a European police office (Europol Convention), OJ C 316, 27/11/1995.
[127] G. VERMEULEN, A judicial counterpart for Europol: should the European Union establish a network of prosecuting and investigating officials?, *Maastricht Journal of European and Comparative Law*, 1997, n° 4, 226-228.
[128] G. VERMEULEN, 1997, 234-235.

investigative methods, is a good example of proactive policing without proper judicial supervision.[129]

112. The increasing European police co-operation gave an international dimension to the principle that police investigations should be supervised and directed. It occurs frequently that several Member States are involved in the investigation of a criminal offence, as well as in the prosecution and trial of the offenders. As a result, conflicts of jurisdiction and a growing risk of forum shopping arise because the intervention of a police force is often a deciding factor in cases where several EU Member States claim jurisdiction to prosecute. In other words: police intervention often determines the location where the suspects are tried and punished. At the moment the police can decide to bring charges in the State where the most important items of evidence can be found or where severe punishment can be expected. Such a situation also affects the legal position of the victims because they could, for example, be unaware of any prosecution or could find themselves forced to bring a civil action in a foreign country.[130]

113. At the Tampere European Council of 15th and 16th October 1999, the European Union wanted to reinforce the fight against serious organised crime by setting up Eurojust, a unit composed of national prosecutors, magistrates, or police officers of equivalent competence, detached from each Member State according to its legal system. The Council has decided, among other things, that Eurojust should facilitate the proper co-ordination of national prosecuting authorities through a central structure.[131] In other words, Eurojust must always guarantee a certain balance between police and judicial co-operation within the framework of the European Union.

114. Since Tampere, the Council has reached broad political agreement on the establishment of Eurojust in the shape of a provisional unit, which from the beginning of 2000 shaped Eurojust in its final form.[132] Pro-Eurojust was established with the following purposes:

- to improve co-operation between the competent national authorities in the investigation and prosecution of serious (organised) crime, involving two or more Member States, and

- to stimulate and to improve the co-ordination of investigations and prosecutions in the Member States, taking into account any request emanating from a competent national authority and any information

---

[129] In the IRT case, the police allowed large amounts of drugs to find their way to the market. The traffic was conducted through an informer, whose access to the police-supplied narcotics was meant to give him credibility within the criminal organisations and to solidify his position within it. This operation lacked proper judicial supervision (G. VERMEULEN, 1997, 235).

[130] G. VERMEULEN, 1997, 241-242.

[131] Tampere European Council of 15 and 16 October 1999, Presidency conclusions, URL://europa.eu.int/council/off/conclu/oct99/oct99_en.htm.

O. LAGODNY, 2001, 131.

[132] CONFERENCE OF THE REPRESENTATIVES OF THE GOVERNMENTS OF THE MEMBER STATES, IGC 2000: Incorporation of a reference to Eurojust in the Treaty, Brussels, 19 November 2000, 2.

provided by any body competent by virtue of provisions adopted within the framework of the Treaties (OLAF, Europol, the European Judicial Network and liaison magistrates).[133]

115. Eurojust should add something new to the existing bodies (e.g. Europol and OLAF) and mechanisms (e.g. European Judicial Network) and must ensure a balanced development of police and judicial co-operation within the European Union.[134] Eurojust will try to bring judicial co-operation up to the level of police co-operation, which has developed much further through Europol.

b.2.2. Analysis of the Powers of Eurojust

116. Eurojust's mission is to stimulate and improve the co-ordination of investigations and prosecutions in the Member States and tries to improve co-operation between the competent authorities of the Member States by facilitating the execution of international mutual legal assistance and the implementation of extradition requests. Eurojust will also support the competent authorities of the Member States in order to render their investigations and prosecutions more effective. Eurojust may also assist in investigations and prosecutions concerning a Member State and a non-Member State where an agreement establishing co-operation pursuant to Article 27(3) has been concluded or where, in a specific case, there is an essential interest in providing such assistance. Finally, Eurojust is competent to assist in investigations and prosecutions concerning only that Member State and the Community, in accordance with the rules laid down by this decision and at the request either of a Member State's competent authority or of the Commission.[135]

117. Eurojust has competence for offences in respect of which Europol is at all times competent to act[136] and for offences such as computer crime, fraud and corruption, and any criminal offence affecting the European Community's financial interests, money laundering, environmental crime, and participation in a criminal organisation. Eurojust can also assist in investigations and prosecutions at the request of a competent authority of a Member State.[137]

118. In order to be able to reach its objectives as efficiently as possible, Eurojust can act through its national members or as a college.[138]

---

[133] Council decision of 14 December 2000 setting up a Provisional Judicial Cooperation Unit, *O.J.*, 21 December 2000, L 324, 2.
[134] COUNCIL OF THE EUROPEAN UNION, Exploratory thoughts concerning Eurojust, Brussels, 4 February 2000, 1.
[135] Council decision of 28 February 2002 setting up Eurojust with a view to reinforcing the fight against serious crime, *O.J.*, 6 March 2002, L 63, 2-3.
[136] Art. 2 of the Europol Convention.
[137] Council decision of 28 February 2002 setting up Eurojust with a view to reinforcing the fight against serious crime, *O.J.*, 6 March 2002, L 63, 3.
[138] Eurojust can act as a college (I) when so requested by one or more of the national members concerned by a case dealt with by Eurojust, or (II) when the case involves investigations or prosecutions which have repercussions at Union level or which might affect Member States other

119. *When Eurojust acts through its national members,* it can ask the competent authorities of the Member States (I) to undertake an investigation or prosecution of specific acts, (II) to accept that another Member State is in a better position to undertake an investigation, (III) to prosecute specific acts, and (IV) to co-ordinate between the competent authorities of the Member States concerned. Furthermore, it can ask (V) to set up a joint investigation team or to provide it with necessary information to carry out its tasks.[139]

120. Eurojust will ensure that the competent authorities of the Member States concerned inform each other of investigations and prosecutions of which it has been informed. It will have power to give assistance to ensure the proper co-ordination of such investigations and prosecutions and to improve co-operation between the competent national authorities. Eurojust will also co-operate and consult with the European Judicial Network and will sometimes assist in investigations and prosecutions done by the competent authorities of a single Member State. Finally, Eurojust may forward requests for judicial assistance (I) made by the competent authority of a Member State, (II) concerning an investigation or prosecution conducted by that authority in a specific case, and (III) impose its intervention with a view to co-ordinated action.[140]

121. There are not so many differences in competence between Eurojust acting through its national members and Eurojust acting as a college.[141] The only differences are that when *Eurojust acts as a college* it will provide assistance in order to improve co-operation between the competent authorities of the Member States, in particular on the basis of Europol's analyses, and that it may assist Europol by providing it with opinions based on those analyses carried out by Europol. Furthermore, it can supply logistical support, which may include assistance in the translation, interpretation, and organisation of co-ordination meetings. If the competent authorities cannot meet a request of Eurojust, they must inform it of their decision and provide the reasons for it. If they are unable to justify it, this could harm essential security interests or jeopardise the success of ongoing investigations or the safety of individuals.[142]

b.2.3. Information

122. *Eurojust* is competent to process personal data by automated means or in structured manual files in order to achieve its objectives and to carry out its

---

than those directly concerned, or (III) when a general question relating to the achievement of its objectives is involved, or (IV) when otherwise provided in the Council decision of 28 February 2002.

[139] Council decision of 28 February 2002 setting up Eurojust with a view to reinforcing the fight against serious crime, *O.J.*, 6 March 2002, L 63, 3.

[140] Council decision of 28 February 2002 setting up Eurojust with a view to reinforcing the fight against serious crime, *O.J.*, 6 March 2002, L 63, 3.

[141] The college shall consist of all the national members and each national member shall have one vote and shall be responsible for the organisation and operation of Eurojust.

[142] Council decision of 28 February 2002 setting up Eurojust with a view to reinforcing the fight against serious crime, *O.J.*, 6 March 2002, L 63, 4.

tasks. Personal data processed by Eurojust must be adequate, relevant, and not excessive. Furthermore, this information must be accurate and up-to-date and must be processed fairly and lawfully.

123. A distinction is made on the one hand between the processing of personal data of persons who are the subject of a criminal investigation or prosecution and, on the other hand, the processing of personal data on persons who are regarded as witnesses or victims in a criminal investigation or prosecution regarding one or more of the types of crime for which Eurojust has competence. In exceptional cases, Eurojust may also process other personal data when such data is necessary for the national investigations concerned as well as for co-ordination within Eurojust.[143] Eurojust will have the competence to maintain an automated data file constituting an index of data relating to investigations in which non-personal data and some forms of personal data[144] may be stored.[145] Eurojust could use this index as an instrument to prevent several countries from enforcing jurisdiction for the same offence. It is important to mention that Eurojust can store personal data as long as necessary for the achievement of its objectives.[146]

124. *Europol* has a computerised system of collected information consisting of an information system (Art. 7 of the Europol Convention), work files established over variable periods of time for the purposes of analysis and containing comprehensive information (Art. 10 of the Europol Convention) and an index system. The information system includes data of persons who are suspected of having committed an offence or where there are serious reasons to believe that they will commit such offences. The work files combine intelligence data from different sources for analytical purposes. The index system is created for the data stored on the work files.[147] The information stored in a Europol database can be very useful for the European body charged with the competence to decide or to recommend which Member State is in the best position to prosecute. In the near future, Europol will need to develop a database of pending investigations[148] preventing any overlap between investigations, and will need to involve several

---

[143] Council decision of 28 February 2002 setting up Eurojust with a view to reinforcing the fight against serious crime, *O.J.*, 6 March 2002, L 63, 5-6.

[144] Art. 15 (1) (a) to (i) and (k) and paragraph 2 of the Council decision of 28 February 2002 setting up Eurojust with a view to reinforcing the fight against serious crime

[145] This index shall be intended to support the management and co-ordination of investigations and prosecutions which Eurojust is assisting, to facilitate access to information on ongoing investigations and prosecutions and to facilitate the monitoring of lawfulness and compliance with the provisions of this Decision concerning the processing of personal data. Furthermore, it shall contain references to temporary work files processed within the framework of Eurojust (Council decision of 28 February 2002 setting up Eurojust with a view to reinforcing the fight against serious crime, *O.J.*, 6 March 2002, L 63, 6).

[146] Council decision of 28 February 2002 setting up Eurojust with a view to reinforcing the fight against serious crime, *O.J.*, 6 March 2002, L 63, 7.

[147] JUSTICE, Submission to the House of Lords European Communities Committee (Sub-Committee F) on European databases, April 1999, 5, URL: www.justice.org.uk/publications/listofpublications/index.html.

[148] See also O. LAGODNY, 2001, 136.

European competent authorities in the same investigation.[149] This database could, on the one hand, be a good instrument to facilitate investigations, but could also be applied for the prevention of multiple prosecutions.

125. Europol and Eurojust have to exchange data in order to contribute to the realisation of the area of freedom, security and justice. Eurojust will forward information to Europol to direct the actions of Europol and Europol will hand over information to Eurojust so that its members can inform the judicial authorities concerned of, for example, cases of money laundering, drug trafficking and human trafficking.[150] It is unclear as to how Europol and Eurojust will exchange this data.

b.2.4. Conclusion

126. Eurojust is only competent to deal with serious forms of international crime and has, in other words, no competence to look into all cases with contact points in more than one State, so States still have to make use of the existing legal instruments or consultation procedures (e.g. transfer of proceedings).

127. Eurojust has the advantage that it works bottom-up and that it can ask the competent authorities of the Member States to accept that another Member State is in a better position to prosecute. This recommendation has a certain value as Eurojust has a lot of authority in practice, but does not alter the fact that it does not have the competence to decide as a judicial authority which State is in the best position to prosecute when there is a conflict of jurisdiction. A decision by Eurojust , in other words, cannot be enforced by the existing mandate. A possible solution could be to provide Eurojust with the power to ask a preliminary question to the European Court of Justice on the question of whether their decision for a certain forum is based on reasonableness. This marginal test should be non-binding. Although it seems that Eurojust's mandate is strong enough, some think that Eurojust should have a decision-making role in judicial matters.[151]

---

[149] Action Plan of 3 December 1998 of the Council and the Commission on how best to implement the provisions of the Treaty of Amsterdam on an area of freedom, security and justice, OJ C 19, 23 January 1999, URL: europa.eu.int/scadplus/leg/en/lvb/l33080.htm; Strategy of 27 March 2000 for the beginning of the new millennium, on the prevention and control of organised crime. In: G. VERMEULEN, 2001, 320.

[150] P. BERTHELET and C. CHEVALLIER-GOVERS, Quelle relation entre Europol et Eurojust? Rapport d'égalité ou rapport d'autorité?, *Revue du Marché commun et de l'Union européenne*, n°450, juillet-août 2001, 471.

[151] JUSTICE, EU co-operation in criminal matters, response to specific proposals, February 2001, 5, URL: www.justice.org.uk/publications/listofpublications/index.html.

2. Trial Phase

a. National Court

128. Most crimes with links in several countries are dealt with at a national level by national authorities. Since the national judge is competent to finish the last stage of prosecution, he should be the appropriate person to determine whether it is well founded that his country is authorised to handle the case and that this decision is not based on unreasonable jurisdiction.[152] He should therefore always check whether the decision on the forum of prosecution does not affect the legal status of the persons concerned (victim and perpetrator).

129. A national judge is not obliged to follow the choices which have been made in the pre-trial phase, even when a European instance has intervened. He can declare himself incompetent, if he thinks that the jurisdiction enforced on his country is not based on reasonableness. Good examples are the Yerodia-case and the case against Ariel Sharon, where the Belgian *Kamer van Inbeschuldigingstelling* has to decide whether Belgium can try Sharon for crimes against humanity on the basis of the genocide law of 1993.

b. European Court of Justice

130. An extension of the competence of the European Court of Justice (Art. 35 of the Treaty of Amsterdam) to give preliminary rulings on jurisdiction matters could be worth considering. The idea is to make a national judge of one of the EU Member States competent to request the Court of Justice to give a preliminary (non-binding) ruling on the question whether his country is in the best position to prosecute, unless Eurojust has already asked such a question.

3. Post-trial Phase

a. European Court of Human Rights

131. Jurisdiction influences the legal status of the victims and the suspects. Consequently, it could be argued that unreasonably enforced jurisdiction could be contrary to Art. 6 of the European Convention on Human Rights. As a result, the European Court of Human Rights could convict a State, at the request of a

---

[152] This negative formulation is important with an eye to the evidence. In this way, the unreasonableness of jurisdiction should be proved. Consequently, it is not up to the State enforcing jurisdiction to provide the evidence that its prosecution is reasonable.

party, for not respecting the rules of fair trial and therefore for enforcing jurisdiction on an arbitrary basis. This is only possible on the condition that this procedure is included in the European Convention on Human Rights.

b. International Court of Justice

132. The International Court of Justice has jurisdiction for all cases which the parties refer to it and all matters specially provided for in the Charter of the United Nations, or in treaties and conventions in force.[153] The relevance for the research is that a State can ask the International Court of Justice to check whether the enforced jurisdiction was contrary to international law. Such an a posteriori control can, for example, be found in the Lotus case and in the Yerodia case.

133. The Lotus case concerned a collision between a French ship ('The Lotus') and a Turkish vessel that has caused the death of several of the Turkish crew. Several people on board the Turkish ship where killed. Negligent behaviour by the officer of the watch of the French ship caused the collision. The French officer had been charged for his actions before a Turkish court. France challenged the Turkish claim, but the permanent Court of International Justice held that the principles of international law do not prevent a state from bringing such charges (judgment No. 9 of 27 September 1927).[154]

134. On 11 April 2000, an investigating judge from the Brussels tribunal de première instance issued "an international arrest warrant in absentia" against Mr. Yerodia, charging him, as perpetrator or co-perpetrator, with offences constituting grave breaches of the Geneva Conventions of 1949 and of the Additional Protocols thereto, and with crimes against humanity. In this Yerodia-case, before the International Court of Justice, the Democratic Republic of the Congo contended that Belgium had violated the "principle that a State may not exercise its authority on the territory of another State", the "principle of sovereign equality among all Members of the United Nations, as laid down in Article 2, paragraph 1, of the Charter of the United Nations", as well as "the diplomatic immunity of the Minister for Foreign Affairs of a sovereign State, as recognised by the jurisprudence of the Court and following from Article 41, paragraph 2, of the Vienna Convention of 18 April 1961 on Diplomatic Relations". The International Court of Justice decided that the arrest warrant of 11 April 2000 constituted violations of a legal obligation of Belgium towards Congo and that Belgium failed to respect the immunity from criminal jurisdiction and the inviolability which the incumbent Minister for Foreign Affairs of Congo enjoyed under international law. Furthermore, Belgium must

---

[153] Art. 36.1 Statute of the International Court of Justice, 25 June 1945, URL: www.icj-cij.org/icjwww/ibasicdocuments/ibasictext/ibasicstatute.htm.
[154] T. VANDER BEKEN, 1999, 5 en 21; COMMISSION OF THE EUROPEAN COMMUNITIES, Mutual Recognition of Decisions in Criminal Matters among the EU Member States and Jurisdiction, Discussion Paper with questions for experts, 2001, 5.

cancel the arrest warrant of 11 April 2000 and inform the authorities to whom that warrant was circulated.[155]

c. European Court of Justice

135. The Corpus Juris prescribes in Art. 28 that the Court of Justice has jurisdiction to rule on offences against the financial interest of the EU. This means an appeal to the European Court is possible at the request of the EPP or a national legal authority on conflicts of jurisdiction regarding application of the rules on the principle of European territoriality, or on the request of the EPP on the exercise of judicial control by national courts. It also includes the competence to pass judgment on the choice of jurisdiction at the request of the accused.[156]

136. The idea of appeal to the court of justice in the post-trial phase could be extended to other offences. Nevertheless, a change in the treaty would be necessary if the Court of Justice was to be made competent regarding crimes against the financial interests of the EU or a broader scope of crimes. This seems unlikely, given the long period of time nations take for ratification.

Part III. Conclusion

137. The problem of conflicts of jurisdiction, driven by prescribing jurisdiction extensively, calls for a clear and efficient approach. Since most crimes with links in several countries are solved at a national level by national authorities, a large number of cases are not visible at international level. As prescribed by Art. 31.d TEU, States should co-operate in order to prevent jurisdiction conflicts, which can be put into practice by limiting national extra-territorial jurisdiction. It is obvious that preventing conflicts of jurisdiction is insufficient, as prevention does not exclude concrete conflicts. Solving conflicts is therefore necessary. This can be achieved by establishing a general and hierarchical list of jurisdiction criteria or by a case by case selection of the most appropriate places for prosecution. Earlier experiences have shown that this hierarchical list is not appropriate, as it is too rigid and mechanical to be suitable for any specific situation and it is not possible to rank the criteria in order of importance. As a result, it is necessary to resort to deliberation, which should always be based on proper administration of justice. The content of this principle is essential and has shifted from mere resocialisation towards a broad application based on reasonableness.

---

[155] INTERNATIONAL COURT OF JUSTICE, case concerning the arrest warrant of 11 April 2000 Democratic Republic of the Congo v. Belgium, 14 February 2002, No. 121.
[156] Corpus Juris 2000, Florence, May 1999, *ERA- forum* 3, 2001, 59.

138. Proper administration of justice calls for a correct balance between the interests of the State and its citizens, because victim and offender cannot merely be treated as legal objects. They have to be considered as legal subjects with rights that can be enforced.

139. In the *pre-trial phase,* attention has been paid to the Convention on Transfer of Proceedings in Criminal Matters, as this convention is an illustration of already existing consultation procedures and because the legal status of the suspect is important in this convention. An intervention by a European body is favourable, as deliberation between States is not institutionalised and does not automatically lead to a solution that can be enforced. It seems that Eurojust is best placed to fulfil the role of consultative body because it works bottom-up and because its mandate foresees the power to ask a State to accept that another Member State is in a better position to prosecute and to co-ordinate between the competent authorities of the Member States concerned. The Corpus Juris project seems to include useful elements. Nevertheless, the competence of the European Prosecutor is restricted to crimes against the financial interests of the EU and the project still needs further development.

140. To ensure the rights of the persons involved, any form of deliberation requires proper judicial control. In the *trial phase* a national judge should always be able to check whether the decision on the forum of prosecution affects the legal status of the persons involved (victim and perpetrator). A possible alternative could be to extend the competence of the European Court of Justice to give preliminary rulings on jurisdiction matters on the request of a national judge of one of the EU Member States.

141. The section concerning the *post-trial phase* has handled the possibility of a higher court to review the enforced jurisdiction. In the research, three different instances have been suggested, being the European Court of Justice, the European Court of Human Rights, and the International Court of Justice. Nevertheless, the first option seems inappropriate, given the fact that it requires a change in the treaty.

142. Furthermore, it could be important for Member States which apply the legality principle to provide for the opportunity to discontinue prosecution with regard to prosecution in another Member State.

143. In conclusion, a comprehensive convention is recommended,[157] including, first of all, the exhortation towards Member States to restrict their prescribing of jurisdiction and subsidiary, to prescribe and enforce only on the basis of reasonable claims. A non-hierarchical list of potentially reasonable criteria, including the principle of territoriality, Art. 8 of the European Convention on Transfer of Proceedings and victim-oriented criteria, seems an appropriate solution that enhances the transparency of the EU legislation. A thorough motivation of any decision regarding the forum choice could promote this

---

[157] A similar initiative has been proposed by OTTO LAGODNY (O. LAGODNY, 2001, 138-142).

transparency. Furthermore, in this convention, the existing international 'ne bis in idem' principle should be given a new and broader content. Finally, it is important that this convention protects the legal interests and status of the suspect and the victim.

Part IV. Recommendation: Draft Convention on the Prevention and Solution of Jurisdiction Conflicts

Preamble

The Member States of the European Union, hereinafter called 'Member States',

Given the close relations between the nations,

Determined to co-operate in the fight against crime, increasingly exceeding the borders of States,

Being of the opinion that, with respect to this matter, it would be useful to establish an agreement at the level of the European Union, in the spirit of mutual confidence, for the prosecution of criminal acts,

Giving expression to faith in the structure and the functioning of each other's legal systems and the ability of all Member States to provide a fair trial,

Guided by the wish to enlarge their co-operation in criminal matters on the basis of mutual confidence, respect and understanding,

Whereas:

(1) Article 31, d of the Treaty of the European Union stipulates that common action on judicial co-operation includes the prevention of conflicts of jurisdiction between the Member States;

(2) Nr. 49 e) of the action Plan of 3 December 1998 of the Council and the Commission on how best to implement the provisions of the Treaty of Amsterdam on an area of freedom, security and justice, recommends the establishment of measures for the co-ordination of criminal investigations and prosecutions in the Member States with the aim of preventing duplication and contradictory rulings, taking account of better use of the 'ne bis in idem' principle;

(3) The Council decision of 28 February 2002 setting up Eurojust with a view to reinforcing the fight against serious crime, more specifically Article 3, describes its mission to stimulate and improve the co-ordination of investigations and prosecutions in the Member States, to improve co-operation between the competent authorities of the Member States, and to support the competent authorities of the Member States in order to render their investigations and prosecutions more effective, and the Articles 6 and

7, defining the tasks of Eurojust, acting through its national members and acting as a College,

HAS DECIDED AS FOLLOWS:

Title I
General Provisions

Article 1
Relationship to other Legal Instruments

The purpose of this Convention is to supplement the provisions and facilitate the application between the Member States of all existing conventions and other legal instruments between Member States concerning judicial co-operation in criminal matters.

Article 2
Provisions Relating to the Schengen acquis

1. The provisions of Articles 5 to 8 constitute measures amending or building upon the provisions referred to in Annex A to the Agreement concluded by the Council of the European Union and the Republic of Iceland and the Kindom of Norway concerning the latters' association with the implementation, application and development of the Schengen acquis.
2. The provisions of Articles 54 to 58 of the Schengen Implementation Convention are hereby repealed.

Article 3
Definitions

For the purpose of this Convention:

a) 'jurisdiction to prescribe' shall mean the legislative competence of a Member State to determine the scope of its criminal law, covering the right of a Member State to establish certain facts as criminal offences and to create criminal law provisions allowing them to sanction infringement of these offences.
b) 'jurisdiction to enforce' shall mean the executive competence to prosecute acts on the basis of the above mentioned provisions to sanction these offences.

Title II
Jurisdiction to prescribe

Article 4
Extraterritorial and Territorial Jurisdiction

Each Member State shall prevent conflicts of jurisdiction by limiting the scope of its extraterritorial jurisdiction unless international legal instruments otherwise define. Additionally, the concept of territoriality shall not be interpreted in the sense that facts that only produce an effect on the territory are considered to be committed on the territory.

Title III
Jurisdiction to enforce

Chapter 1
Ne bis in idem

Article 5
Final Sentence

A person who has been finally judged in a Member State may not be prosecuted in another Member State in respect of the same facts:
a) if he was acquitted;
b) if the sanction imposed:

    i) has been completely enforced or is being enforced, or

    ii) has been wholly, or with respect to the part not enforced, the subject of a pardon or an amnesty, or

    iii) can no longer be enforced because of a lapse of time;
c) if the court convicted the person without imposing a sanction.

Article 6
Irrevocable Settlement

Nobody can be prosecuted in a Member State because of a fact that has been settled irrevocably in another Member State with respect to that person, by the satisfaction of a specific condition, imposed by the competent authorities of the latter Member State, preventing prosecution.

Article 7
Information

1. If a criminal charge is brought against a person in a Member State and the competent authorities of that Member State have reason to believe that this charge concerns the same facts as those for which he has been finally judged or

that have been settled irrevocably by the satisfaction of a specific condition in another Member State, they shall, if they consider it necessary, request the relevant information from the competent authorities of the concerned Member State or from bodies set up pursuant to the Treaty on European Union.

2. The information requested shall be given as soon as possible and shall be taken into account in determining whether the proceedings should be continued.

3. Each Member State shall, at the time of signature, ratification, acceptance, or approval of this Convention, specify the authorities authorised to request and receive information under this article.

Article 8
Wider National Provisions

The above provisions shall not preclude the application of wider national provisions on the 'ne bis in idem' effect attached to legal decisions taken abroad.

Chapter 2
Proper Administration of Justice

Article 9
Unreasonable Enforcement of Jurisdiction

In order to attain a proper administration of justice, Member States shall not enforce jurisdiction when this is unreasonable. The enforcement of jurisdiction by a Member State is manifestly unreasonable if this is not the Member State:

1. where the offence has been committed;
2. where the suspected person is ordinarily resident;
3. of the nationality or the origin of the suspected person;
4. where the suspected person is undergoing or is to undergo a sentence involving deprivation of liberty;
5. where proceedings for the same or other offences are being taken against the suspected person by its prosecuting authorities;
6. where the most important items of evidence are located;
7. where the enforcement of a possible future sentence is likely to improve the prospects for the social rehabilitation of the person sentenced;
8. where the presence of the suspected person at the hearing of proceedings can be guaranteed;
9. where a possible future sentence can be enforced;
10. where the injured person is ordinarily resident;
11. of the nationality or the origin of the injured person or
12. where damage has occurred.

Article 10
National Authorities

If several Member States have jurisdiction over certain acts and without prejudice to Article 30 to 33 of the European Convention of 15 May 1972 on the transfer of proceedings in criminal matters, the competent legal authorities of each Member State shall co-operate to agree on which Member State or Member States are in a reasonable position to enforce jurisdiction.

Article 11
Eurojust

When fulfilling its tasks prescribed by Article 6 of the Council Decision of 28 February 2002 setting up Eurojust with a view to reinforcing the fight against serious crime, Eurojust will promote the reasonable enforcement of jurisdiction.

Article 12
National Judge

Any court or tribunal of a Member State may request the European Court of Justice to give a preliminary ruling on a question raised in a case pending before it concerning whether enforcement of jurisdiction on its country is unreasonable if that court or tribunal considers that a decision on the question is necessary to enable it to give judgement.

Title IV
Judicial Co-operation in Criminal Matters

Article 13

1. A Member State will not comply with a request for mutual legal assistance from another Member State if the procedure which gave rise to the request involves a person who has already been acquitted in a Member State of the same criminal charges as those which gave rise to the request, or, in the event of a conviction, no sentence was passed on the person involved, or he or she has already served the sentence or is still serving the sentence, or he can no longer be subject to the enforcement of the sentence under the law of that Member State on account of pardon, amnesty, or prescription of lapse of time.
2. A Member State will not comply with a request for mutual legal assistance from another Member State if the facts which gave rise to the request have already been irrevocably dealt with in a Member State by the satisfaction of a certain condition.
3. A Member State is entitled to refuse to comply with a request for mutual legal assistance from another Member State, if the procedure which gave rise to the request involves a person who has already been acquitted in a non-Member State of the same criminal charges as those which gave rise to the request, or, in the

event of a conviction, no sentence was passed on the person involved, or he has already served the sentence or is still serving the sentence, or he can no longer be subject to the enforcement of the sentence under the law of that State on account of pardon, amnesty, or prescription of lapse of time.

4. A Member State is entitled to refuse to comply with a request for mutual legal assistance from another Member State if the facts which gave rise to the request have already been irrevocably dealt with in a non-Member State by the satisfaction of a certain condition.

5. This article enlarges the grounds for refusal for judicial co-operation in criminal matters, as prescribed in the existing conventions.

Title V
Final provisions

Article 14
Reservations

No reservation may be entered in respect of this Convention.

Article 15
Territorial Application

This Convention shall apply to Gibraltar.

Article 16
Entry into Force

1. This Convention shall be subject to adoption by the Member States in accordance with their respective constitutional requirements.

2. Member States shall notify the Secretary-General of the Council of the European Union of the completion of the constitutional procedures for the adoption of this Convention.

3. This Convention shall, 90 days after the notification referred to in paragraph 2 by the State, member of the European Union at the time of adoption by the Council of the Act establishing this Convention, which is the eighth to complete this formality, enter into force for the eight Member States concerned.

4. Any notification by a Member State subsequent to the receipt of the eighth notification referred to in paragraph 2 shall have the effect that, 90 days after the subsequent notification, this convention shall enter into force as between this Member State and those Member States for which the Convention has already entered into force.

5. Before the Convention has entered into force pursuant to paragraph 3, any Member State may, when giving the notification referred to in paragraph 2 or at any time thereafter, declare that it will apply this Convention in its relations with Member States which have made the same declaration. Such declarations shall take effect 90 days after the date of deposit thereof.

6. This Convention shall apply to facts whereby no final decision has been made on the date this Convention enters into force in the Member States involved or is applied on account of paragraph 5.

Article 17
Accession of New Member States

1. This Convention shall be open to accession by any State which becomes a Member of the European Union.
2. The text of this Convention in the language of the acceding State, drawn up by the Council of the European Union, shall be authentic.
3. The instruments of accession shall be deposited with the depositary.
4. This Convention shall enter into force with respect to any State which accedes to it ninety days after the deposit of its instrument of accession or on the date of entry into force of this Convention if it has not already entered into force at the time of expiry of the said period of ninety days.
5. Where this Convention is not yet in force at the time of the deposit of their instrument of accession, Article 16 paragraph 5 shall apply to acceding Member States.

Article 18
Entry into Force for Iceland and Norway

1. Without prejudice to Article 8 of the Agreement concluded by the Council of the European Union and the Republic of Iceland and the Kingdom of Norway concerning the latters' association with the implementation, application and development of the Schengen acquis (the 'Association Agreement'), the provisions referred to in Article 2(1) shall enter into force for Iceland and Norway 90 days after the receipt by the Council and the Commission of the information pursuant to Article 8(2) of the Association Agreement upon fulfilment of their constitutional requirements, in their mutual relations with any Member State for which this Convention has already entered into force pursuant to Article 27(3) or (4).
2. Any entry into force of this Convention for a Member State after the date of entry into force of the provisions referred to in Article 2(1) for Iceland and Norway, shall render these provisions also applicable in the mutual relations between that Member State and Iceland and Norway.
3. The provisions referred to in Article 2(1) shall in any event not become binding on Iceland and Norway before the date to be fixed pursuant to Article 15(4) of the Association Agreement.
4. Without prejudice to paragraphs 1, 2 and 3 above, the provisions referred to in Article 2(1) shall enter into force for Iceland and Norway not later than on the date of entry into force of this Convention for the fifteenth State, being a member of the European Union at the time of the adoption by the Council of the Act establishing this Convention.

Article 19
Depositary

1. The Secretary-General of the Council of the European Union shall act as depositary of this Convention.

2. The depositary shall publish in the Official Journal of the European Communities information on the progress of adoptions and accessions, statements and reservations, and also any other notification concerning this Convention.

Part V. Executive summary

The internationalisation of crime and criminal justice has induced several problems. During the last few decades, countries have extended the application of their national criminal law to crimes which are committed outside their territory in order to prevent certain States from developing into 'safe havens' for criminals. This evolution towards more extra-territorial jurisdiction has created situations in which more than one State can claim jurisdiction.

Given the fact that most crimes with links in several countries are dealt with on a national level by national authorities, a large number of cases are not visible at an international level. And so, it is only where more than one State enforces jurisdiction that concrete conflicts of jurisdiction emerge. These conflicts have significant consequences for the States and the individuals involved. Not only criminal law, but also criminal procedure law differ from country to country. The assignment of a case to a foreign country can therefore be detrimental to the offender's legal status. For instance, a German sentenced in Spain is unfamiliar with the Spanish language, law and culture.

In order to contribute to the enhancement of an area of freedom, security, and justice within the European Union, this paper has analysed whether the prevention or solution of conflicts of jurisdiction is possible, how these matters can be applied, and what contribution the European Union can make. The pursued goal was a realistic, short-term solution, which means that certain tracks, like the establishment of a European Criminal Court and a single European penal law, have not been addressed. Since the jurisdiction problem is inherent in all criminal justice systems of both the common law and civil law type, the aim of the research was to create a system on a reasonable basis that is applicable to all States, with specific attention to the rights of the persons involved.

In this study a division has been made between jurisdiction to prescribe, which is a legislative competence, and jurisdiction to enforce, which is an executive competence.

Currently, finding a State that has jurisdiction is easier than pointing one out that has no jurisdiction. This can be explained by the fact that many States are convinced that they should prescribe jurisdiction not only for offences which have been committed on their own territory, but also for crimes committed outside their territory. As a result, conflicts of jurisdiction are inevitable because too many States are in a position to start prosecution.

Two sorts of jurisdiction can be distinguished. These are primary and derivative jurisdiction, each of which contains several contact points. The first one is based directly on the national field of application (territoriality principle, active and passive personality principle, protection principle, and universality principle), while the latter occurs when jurisdiction is derived from a competent state (substitution and adoption of proceedings).

The *territoriality principle* is accepted everywhere as the first and most important contact point when the authority of a State to prescribe jurisdiction over acts that take place on its own territory is uncontested. As a consequence of the fact that both civil law countries and common law countries give a broad interpretation to the concept of territory, it is possible that several States will consider themselves competent to start prosecution on the basis of this principle. A possible solution for conflicts could therefore be the application of a more restricted definition of the concept of 'territory'.

Besides the 'locus delicti', States can also apply one of the *principles of extraterritorial jurisdiction* to start prosecution. These principles enable States to prescribe jurisdiction for offences, which cannot be located on their own territory. This form of prosecution is mostly subsidiary to the 'locus delicti'.

While the aforementioned principles are based on strong contact points that allow States to prescribe and enforce jurisdiction unilaterally, States lacking such a contact point are sometimes able to enforce jurisdiction derived from a State that has one of the original contact points with the crime. *Substitution* is based on the 'aut dedere aut iudicare' principle and is inextricably linked with extradition. On the basis of this concept, a State decides to start prosecution in situations where they do not extradite a foreigner. Substitution can have significant consequences for suspects and victims of criminal offences, as prosecution could come as a complete surprise for them, although there are some guarantees (e.g. the requirement of double incrimination). The suspect may consequently be tried in a country in which he did not expect to be prosecuted at the moment he has committed the crimes. Jurisdiction on the basis of substitution could also create confusion for the victim because his case could be dealt with in an 'unknown' State.

Adoption of proceedings is the second form of derivative jurisdiction and is dependent on a specific request by a State that has original jurisdiction. The concept is inspired by a proper administration of justice. In these cases a State enforces jurisdiction not because it can justify a strong contact point, but because it is in the best position to do so. The onus is on the State that considers another State to be in a better position to take over prosecution, and not on the State that will eventually enforce jurisdiction . Parallel to substitution, the adoption of proceedings has an important impact on the legal status of the persons involved. At the moment, the determination of the place of the trial is a barely predictable policy decision for both, instead of a clear matter of criminal law and criminal procedure.

Two suggestions are proposed regarding the predictability of the instrument of adoption of proceedings and to avoid forum shopping. According to the first view, a foregoing determination in a treaty of general criteria of proper administration of justice is sufficient to cope with the requirements of foreseeability and certainty. The second suggestion is to involve the suspect and the victim more closely in this procedure, as proper administration of justice is too vague and weak as a contact point for jurisdiction. Suspects and victims must be treated as persons with a place and a voice and must therefore have a decisive influence on this transfer and adoption procedure to justify prosecution. The second suggestion seems more consistent in substance.

The instrument of adoption of proceedings is, in practice, not very attractive for States as it creates more work and it is based on solidarity. Furthermore, the result is that people are prosecuted, although the State does not want or cannot prosecute on its own initiative because there is no real contact point.

Generally, there is a clear trend among Member States to prescribe jurisdiction on a large scale. The EU seems to stimulate this since the first priority set forth in many legal papers is to prescribe jurisdiction. This is contrary to the aim of Art 31.d TEU according to which the EU wants to prevent conflicts of jurisdiction. Instead of stimulating Member States to prescribe jurisdiction, it might consequently be recommended that the EU gives a clear message to the States to temper their jurisdiction policy. This recommendation could prevent a number of jurisdiction conflicts in the future.

Although abstract conflicts of jurisdiction can partly be avoided if States prescribe jurisdiction in a restricted way, a large number of conflicts will be left unsolved since overlaps of jurisdiction are still possible. A system of exclusive territorial jurisdiction seems to be an unrealistic option, as this requires a fundamental political change.

The restraint on prescribing jurisdiction in itself is not sufficient, since concrete conflicts can also emerge at the level of the enforcement of jurisdiction: States are free to decide not to prosecute even though they are competent, since the division implies both the attraction and the repulsion of cases.

Currently, a concrete conflict of jurisdiction is solved by (a) unilateral action of the States, which results in pushing the conflict to extremes and the persistency of the prosecution by several States, or (b) deliberation or compliance with the international 'ne bis in idem principle'. Since the first option is not to be supported in a European area of freedom, security, and justice and is not to be recommended, we will focus our analyses on the amicable solution of conflicts by deliberation and respect for the 'ne bis in idem' principle.

Several initiatives to introduce an *international ne bis in idem principle* have been taken by different institutions, some more fruitful than others. A study of these treaties shows that this principle is widely recognised at international level. Even if the universal 'ne bis in idem principle' is not yet generally accepted, it is clear that important progress has already been made.

Still, the existence of several gaps of the international 'ne bis in idem' principle give rise to additional jurisdiction problems. The most substantial criticism of the existing 'ne bis' principle is its narrow application within the EU. Paragraph 54 of the Schengen Implementing Convention is only relevant to final decisions, although it seems more appropriate to expand the concept to other decisions, such as the decision not to prosecute, the decision to provide immunity of prosecution, alternative settlement, and dismissal.

The idea of a broader 'ne bis in idem' principle should be correlated to mutual legal assistance since the 'ne bis' principle currently provides no absolute grounds for the refusal of mutual legal assistance. It is contradictory to prohibit a second prosecution for facts that have already been judged, but at the same time to allow mutual legal assistance, such as extradition, concerning that offender. In order to avoid co-operation between States that can lead to an infraction of this principle, mutual legal assistance is to be put on the same level as decisions.

This goes hand in hand with the regrettable absence of a European criminal record database, since for the moment it is hardly possible for a State to be aware of the fact that there has been a decision concerning a certain case in another State.

A second option to solve concrete conflicts of jurisdiction is to restrain the exercise of jurisdiction by *deliberation*. This limitation can be established in two different ways, which should be based on the proper administration of justice.

It is important to stress that the concept of proper administration of justice does not necessarily imply swift and effective justice. A balance is required between the necessity of prosecution and humanitarian considerations such as resocialisation of the accused, prosecution in a country where the accused is familiar with the law and the language, the interests of the victim etc. Proper administration also covers considerations of criminal proceeding (e.g. prevention of double prosecution, avoiding sentence by default,...).

The first option is to build in a hierarchy in the claims of jurisdiction so that it can be decided by virtue of a treaty which State is in the best position to prosecute.However, the efforts to set up a list of criteria were not very fruitful, since such a hierarchical solution seemed too inflexible and mechanical to be suitable for any specific situation. A list of criteria is consequently still considered as unfeasible and undesirable.

The second view, advocated in this paper, starts with the idea that it is impossible to structure these claims hierarchically because the decision should be examined case by case. An alternative solution is proposed, starting with an analysis of the applicable criteria on which a judgment should be based. Furthermore, attention will be paid to several organisational requirements that are necessary for deliberation and control, making a distinction between the different stages of the proceedings, being the pre-trial phase, the trial phase, and the post-trial phase.

In the context of deliberation, it is important to draw attention to the subsidiarity principle, which means that not every case with contact points in more than one State can be deliberated at a European level, such as, for example, a Belgian who commits shoplifting in the Netherlands. Such a case falls into the hands of a national prosecutor and will probably never reach the discussion at an international level.

In addition, attention should be paid to the option of splitting up and merging certain cases, specifically in the framework of joint investigations. The question whether it is preferable to concentrate the committals for trial in a single Member State or to assign different components of a complex case to various countries, and the problem of which country should consequently be competent for the prosecution, should be answered on an identical base as other crimes with links in various countries.

Deliberation can be based on two sorts of criteria, and these are positive and negative criteria. Positive criteria of any kind are mentioned in various international treaties and judgments. For instance, Art. 8 of the European Convention on the Transfer of Proceedings in Criminal Matters (1972) indicates the cases in which one contracting State may request the proceedings in another contracting State and is used in several other conventions:

1. *the suspected person is ordinarily resident in the requested State;*
2. *the suspected person is a national of the requested State or if that State is his State of origin;*
3. *the suspected person is undergoing or is to undergo a sentence involving deprivation of liberty in its territory;*
4. *proceedings for the same or other offences are being taken against the suspected person by its prosecuting authorities;*
5. *the most important items of evidence are located in its territory;*
6. *the enforcement in its territory of a possible future sentence is likely to improve the prospects for the social rehabilitation of the person sentenced;*
7. *unlike in the requesting State, the presence of the suspected person can be ensured at the hearing of proceedings in its territory or*
8. *unlike the requesting State, it could enforce a possible future sentence.*

The Corpus Juris has also devoted Article 26 § 2 to the forum choice, listing non-hierarchically:

1.the State where the greater part of evidence is found;
2.the State of residence or of nationality of the accused (or the principal persons accused);
3.the State where the economic impact of the offence is the greatest.'

The European Convention on the Transfer of Proceedings and the Corpus Juris both enlist positive criteria. Nevertheless, it seems more fruitful to focus on the negative criteria. This could, for instance, be the case if the criterion of the harshest punishment is decisive. The analysis of the positive and negative criteria leads to the view that the traditional criteria are necessary for the exercise of jurisdiction, but not sufficient. An additional requirement, already developed by the American Law Institute, could be the reasonableness in concreto of the enforcement of jurisdiction. Jurisdiction based on impermissible criteria should be prohibited in any case. This reasonable enforcement of jurisdiction is in line with the existing 'abuse of process' in common law, and the German 'Abwägungsfehlerlehre'.

It seems appropriate to create a non-hierarchical list of potentially reasonable criteria in order to enhance the transparency of EU legislation. This list could contain the principle of territoriality, Art. 8 of the European Convention on Transfer of Proceedings and victim oriented criteria, such as the ordinary residence, the nationality or the origin of the victim, or the territory on which the damage has occured. The completion of negative criteria could be left to the competent judicial bodies, by means of a praetorian development. These could be used as prosecution guidelines, enhancing transparency by means of their public character. A thorough motivation, which mentions the applied criteria, seems essential, no matter which body decides on the forum choice.

During the pre-trial phase, deliberation is possible at a national level by a consultation between national authorities. Several EU instruments already foresee a consultation procedure at a national level, such as the European Convention of 15 May 1972 on the Transfer of Proceedings in Criminal Matters, which pays attention to the legal status of the persons involved and provides them with certain guarantees. The Nordic States also have a consultation mechanism, based on trust, which is comparable to the procedure laid down in the European Convention on the Transfer of Proceedings.

Nevertheless, an intervention by a European body like a European Public Prosecutor or Eurojust is positive, as deliberation between States is not institutionalised and does not automatically lead to a solution that can be compelled.

The Corpus Juris, set up for the protection of the financial interests of the European Union, seems to give an adequate framework in terms of competence of jurisdiction. In order to conduct investigations for these specific kinds of crime, a European Public Prosecutor has been proposed (EPP), who is deemed suitable to decide on the forum choice.

The allocation of jurisdiction to one Member State by the EPP may have certain implications with regard to Member States' international obligations since these may contain agreements concerning the establishment of jurisdiction for certain cases that are contradictory to his decision. On the other hand, this decision has several advantages. First of all, it will be much easier for the other Member States to recognise and therefore accept that State's sentence compared to a situation where their own authorities would also have been competent to decide. Forum shopping, by either the prosecution or the defence, could be prevented. Furthermore, there would be less of a risk of 'ne bis in idem' situations arising.

As regards the review of the choice of a Member State of trial by the EPP, two possible options have been suggested. The first one, based on trust in all the national legal systems, is to make him entirely responsible for the choice. This can be detrimental to the offender if the court is selected on an unfair basis, since the EPP would in this case have the discretionary power which he needs. A second option is to entrust the review function to the double supervision of the judge of freedoms and the national court.

The idea has been launched to entrust the control of the EPP to a European preliminary chamber at the moment of the closing of the preliminary investigation in order to avoid an a posteriori control. This preliminary chamber has been suggested because of several shortcomings in the original proposition. First of all, the national judge of freedoms will often have to deal with a part of the procedure that has taken place in a foreign country. Consequently the hypothesis that this judge has to apply foreign law in addition to his own law and the Corpus Juris is not unreal. A second disadvantage is that forum shopping is possible by the EPP on the hypothesis that several judges of freedoms were caught.

This chamber could be composed of judges from the European Court of Justice or could be a newly established organ, which receives the prejudicial questions of the national judge of freedoms. Whether these questions can be raised by the EPP or a citizen is not clear. Although the option of a preliminary chamber seems feasible, it is no longer mentioned in the Green Paper.

The proposal to provide the EPP with the power to decide on the forum choice has the theoretical advantage that it is problem solving, as the decision of the EPP can be compelled. However, there seem to be more disadvantages. First of all, the Corpus Juris project is a rather immature concept, based on a fictive European territory. Further, it is only set up for the protection of the financial interests of the European Union. Finally, the Corpus Juris functions top-down and intervenes too strongly in the positive injunction power of the Member States.

A second option is to let Eurojust intervene during the pre-trial phase. It is composed of national prosecutors, magistrates, or police officers of equivalent competence, detached from each Member State. At the Tampere European Council, the decision was made to set up this body in order to facilitate the proper co-ordination of national prosecuting authorities through a central structure. This includes the task of ensuring a certain balance between police and judicial co-operation within the framework of the European Union.

In order to reach its objectives as efficiently as possible, Eurojust can act through its national members or as a college. When Eurojust acts through its national members it can ask the competent authorities of the Member States (I) to undertake an investigation or prosecution of specific acts, (II) to accept that another Member State is in a better position to undertake an investigation, (III) to prosecute specific acts, and (IV) to co-ordinate between the competent authorities of the Member States concerned. Furthermore, it can ask (V) to set up a joint investigation team or to provide it with necessary information to carry out its tasks. The competence of Eurojust acting as a college is approximately parallel.

Information gathering is of crucial importance for any decision made by Eurojust. Therefore, co-operation with Europol is necessary in order to contribute to the realisation of the area of freedom, security and justice.

Eurojust is only competent to deal with serious forms of international crime. This includes the offences in respect of which Europol is always competent to act and offences like computer crime, fraud and corruption and any criminal offence affecting the European Community's financial interests, money laundering, environmental crime, and participation in a criminal organisation. As a consequence of this limitation, States still have to make use of the existing legal instruments or consultation procedures (e.g. transfer of proceedings).

Eurojust has the advantage that it works bottom-up and that it can ask the competent authorities of the Member States to accept that another Member State is in a better position to prosecute. This recommendation has a certain value as Eurojust has a lot of authority in practice, but does not alter the fact that it does not have the competence to decide as a judicial authority which State is in the best position to prosecute when there is a conflict of jurisdiction. A decision of Eurojust , in other words, cannot be compelled within the existing mandate. A possible solution could be to provide Eurojust with the power to ask a preliminary question to the European Court of Justice on the question of whether their decision for a certain forum is based on reasonableness. This marginal test should be non-binding. Although it seems that Eurojust's mandate is strong enough, some think that Eurojust should have a decision-making role in judicial matters.

The second stage of procedure in which crimes can be allocated is the trial phase. Currently, most crimes with links in several countries are dealt with on a national level by national authorities. Since the national judge is competent to finish the last stage of prosecution, he should be the appropriate person to determine whether it is well founded that his country is authorised to handle the case and that this decision is not based on unreasonably enforced jurisdiction. He should always check whether or not the decision on the forum of prosecution affects the legal status of the persons concerned. A national judge is not obliged to follow the choices which have been made in the pre-trial phase, even when a European instance has intervened. He is allowed to declare himself incompetent when he thinks that the jurisdiction enforced on his country is not based on reasonably enforced jurisdiction.

Nevertheless, an extension of the competence of the European Court of Justice (Art. 35 of the Treaty of Amsterdam) to give preliminary rulings on jurisdiction matters could be worth considering. The idea is to make a national judge from one of the EU Member States competent to request the Court of Justice to give a preliminary (non-binding) ruling on the question of whether or not his country is in the best position to prosecute, unless Eurojust has already asked such a question.

Thirdly, the post-trial phase provides opportunities to review the decision on which country is competent to prosecute. Given the fact that this decision influences the legal status of the victims and the suspects, it could be argued that unreasonably enforced jurisdiction is an infringement of Art. 6 of the European Convention on Human Rights. The European Court of Human Rights could therefore convict a State at the request of a party, for not respecting the rules of fair trial and for enforcing jurisdiction on an arbitrary basis.

The International Court of Justice also has a part to play during the post-trial phase. This court has jurisdiction for all cases which the parties refer to it and all matters specially provided for in the Charter of the United Nations, or in treaties and conventions in force. The relevance for the research is that a State can ask the International Court of Justice to check whether the enforced jurisdiction was contrary to international law.

A third proposal during the post-trial phase is to create an appeal procedure to the European Court of Justice. The Corpus Juris prescribes in Art. 28 that the European Court of Justice has jurisdiction to rule on offences against the financial interest of the EU. This means an appeal is possible at the request of the EPP or a national legal authority on conflicts of jurisdiction regarding application of the rules on the principle of European territoriality, or on the request of the EPP on the exercise of judicial control by national courts. It also includes the competence to pass judgment on the choice of jurisdiction at the request of the accused.

The idea of appeal to the Court of Justice in the post-trial phase could be extended to other offences. Nevertheless, a change of treaty would be necessary if the Court of Justice were to be made competent regarding crimes against the financial interests of the EU or a broader scope of crimes. This does not seem realistic, given the long period of time nations take for ratification.

In conclusion, a comprehensive convention is recommended, including, first of all, the exhortation towards Member States to restrict their prescribing of jurisdiction and subsidiary, to prescribe and enforce only on the basis of reasonable claims. A non-hierarchical list of potentially reasonable criteria, including the principle of territoriality, Art. 8 of the European Convention on Transfer of Proceedings and victim-oriented criteria, seems an appropriate solution that enhances the transparency of the EU legislation. A thorough motivation of any decision regarding the forum choice could promote this transparency. Furthermore, in this convention the existing international 'ne bis in idem' principle should be given a new and broader content. Finally, it is important that this convention protects the legal interests and status of the suspect and the victim.

Part VI. Synthèse

L'internationalisation de la criminalité et de la justice pénale a généré plusieurs problèmes. Au cours des dernières décennies, les pays ont étendu l'application de leur droit pénal à des crimes commis en-dehors de leur territoire afin d'éviter que certains Etats ne deviennent des « havres de paix » pour les criminels. Cette évolution vers une compétence plus extra-territoriale a induit des situations dans lesquelles plus d'un Etat peut établir compétence.

Etant donné que la plupart des crimes liés à plusieurs pays sont pris en charge au niveau national par les autorités nationales, un grand nombre de cas ne sont pas visibles au niveau international. Par conséquent, lorsque plus d'un pays applique une compétence, des conflits de compétence concrets apparaissent. Ces conflits ont des conséquences importantes pour les Etats et les individus concernés. Le droit pénal, mais aussi la procédure pénale, diffèrent d'un pays à l'autre. La cession d'un cas à un pays étranger peut donc être préjudiciable au statut juridique du criminel. Par exemple, un Allemand condamné en Espagne n'est pas familier de la langue, des lois et de la culture espagnoles.

Afin de contribuer à l'amélioration d'un espace de liberté, de sécurité et de justice au sein de l'Union Européenne, le présent article a procédé à l'analyse du fait de savoir si la prévention ou la résolution des conflits de compétences était possible, comment on pouvait y arriver dans la pratique et quelle pouvait être la contribution de l'Union Européenne. L'objectif visé était une solution à court terme réaliste, ce qui signifie que certains points, comme la création d'un tribunal pénal européen et d'un droit pénal européen, n'ont pas été abordés. Etant donné que le problème de compétence est inhérent à tous les systèmes de justice pénales (à la fois au 'common law' et au droit civil), l'objectif de la recherche était de créer un système sur une base raisonnable et applicable à tous les Etats, avec une attention particulière aux droits des personnes concernées.

Dans cette étude, une division a été opérée entre la compétence législative, et la compétence juridictionelle.

A l'heure actuelle, il est plus facile de trouver un Etat compétent que d'en trouver un qui n'en est pas. Cela peut s'expliquer par le fait que de nombreux Etats sont convaincus qu'ils devraient être compétent non seulement pour les crimes commis sur leur propre territoire, mais également pour les crimes commis en-dehors de leur territoire. Par conséquent, les conflits de compétence sont inévitables, parce que trop d'Etats sont à même de lancer des poursuites judiciaires.

Il convient de distinguer deux types de compétence : la compétence primaire et la compétence subsidiaire, chacune comportant plusieurs points de contact. La première repose directement sur le domaine d'application national (principe de territorialité, principe de personnalité active et passive, principe de protection et principe d'universalité), tandis que la seconde survient lorsque la compétence est dérivée d'un Etat compétent (substitution et adoption de procédures).

Le *principe de territorialité* est accepté partout comme étant le premier et le plus important point de contact lorsque l'autorité d'un Etat établissant une compétence pour des actes ayant eu lieu sur son propre territoire est incontestée. Conséquence du fait que les pays de type 'common law' et les pays de type droit civil donnent une vaste interprétation du concept de territoire, il est possible que plusieurs Etats se considèrent compétents pour lancer des poursuites judiciaires sur base de ce principe. Une solution possible à ces conflits pourrait par conséquent être l'application d'une définition plus réduite du concept de « territoire ».

Outre le lieu où le crime a été commis, des Etats peuvent également appliquer l'un des *principes de compétence extraterritoriale* pour lancer des poursuites. Ces principes permettent aux Etats d'appliquer une compétence juridictionelle pour des crimes ne pouvant être situés sur leur propre territoire. Cette forme de poursuite est principalement subsidiaire au lieu du crime.

Alors que les principes précités reposent sur de forts points de contact permettant aux Etats de recommander et d'appliquer unilatéralement une compétence, les Etats manquant d'un tel point de contact sont parfois à même d'appliquer une compétence dérivée d'un Etat possédant un point de contact originel avec le crime. La *substitution* repose sur le principe « *aut dedere aut iudicare* » et est inextricablement liée à l'extradition. Sur base de ce concept, un Etat peut décider de lancer des poursuites judiciaires dans des situations où il ne procède pas à l'extradition d'un étranger. La substitution peut avoir d'importantes conséquences pour les suspects et les victimes de faits punissables, car les poursuites judiciaires peuvent s'avérer être une totale surprise pour eux, même s'il existe certaines garanties (la nécessité d'une double incrimination). Par conséquent, le suspect peut être jugé dans un pays dans lequel il ne s'attendait pas à être poursuivi au moment où il a perpétré des faits punissables. La compétence reposant sur la substitution peut également engendrer une certaine confusion pour la victime, parce que son cas pourrait être traité par un Etat « inconnu ».

L'*adoption de procédures* est la deuxième forme de compétence subsidiaire et dépend d'une requête concrète d'un Etat ayant une compétence originelle. Ce concept est inspiré par une bonne administration de la justice. En pareils cas, un Etat applique une compétence non pas parce qu'il peut justifier d'un solide point de contact, mais parce qu'il est dans la meilleure position pour le faire. L'accent est mis sur l'Etat qui considère un autre Etat comme étant mieux à même de lancer les poursuites judiciaires, et non sur l'Etat qui applique en fin de compte la compétence. Parallèlement à la substitution, l'adoption de procédure possède un impact considérable sur le statut juridique des personnes concernées. A l'heure actuelle, la détermination du lieu du procès est une décision difficilement prévisible pour les deux, et il n'est nullement question d'une affaire claire de droit pénal et de procédures pénales.

Deux possibilités sont proposées pour ce qui est de la prévisibilité de l'instrument d'adoption de procédures et afin d'éviter une course au plus offrant. Selon la première possibilité, la détermination préalable dans un traité des critères généraux d'une bonne administration de la justice suffit pour se charger des exigences de prévisibilité et de certitude. La seconde possibilité est d'impliquer davantage le prévenu et la victime dans cette procédure, car la bonne administration de la justice est trop vague et constitue un point de contact trop faible pour la compétence. Les prévenus et les victimes doivent être traités en tant que personnes ayant une place et une voix, et doivent donc avoir une influence décisive sur ce transfert et sur la procédure d'adoption pour justifier les poursuites. La seconde possibilité semble plus logique en substance.

L'instrument d'adoption de procédures n'est en pratique pas attrayant pour les Etats, car il génère plus de travail et parce qu'il repose sur la solidarité. En outre, le résultat est que des gens sont poursuivis en justice, bien que l'Etat ne veule ou ne puisse entamer des poursuites judiciaires de sa propre initiative parce qu'il n'existe pas de point de contact réel.

En général, il y a une tendance claire parmi les Etats Membres à établir la compétence législative à grande échelle. L'UE semble stimuler cela, étant donné que la première priorité présentée dans de nombreux instruments juridiques est d'établir la compétence législative. Cela est contraire à l'objectif de l'article 31.d TEU selon lequel l'UE veut éviter les conflits de compétence. Plutôt que stimuler les Etats Membres à établir une compétence législative, il serait par conséquent recommandé que l'UE transmette aux Etats un message clair visant à tempérer leur politique juridictionnelle. Cette recommandation permettrait à l'avenir d'éviter certain conflits de compétence.

Bien que les conflits de compétence abstraits puissent partiellement être évités si les Etats établissent la competence législative de façon réduite, un grand nombre de conflits resteront non résolus étant donné que les chevauchements de compétence restent possibles. Un système de compétence territoriale exclusive semble être une option irréalisable, car elle nécessiterait un changement politique fondamental.

La contrainte sur l'établissement de la compétence législative n'est en elle-même pas efficace, car des conflits concrets peuvent également survenir au niveau de l'application de la compétence : les Etats sont libres de décider de ne pas poursuivre même s'ils sont compétents pour le faire, car la division implique l'attraction et la répulsion des cas.

A l'heure actuelle, un conflit de compétence concret est résolu (a) par une action unilatérale des Etats, ce qui revient à pousser le conflit à des extrêmes et à la persistance des poursuites par plusieurs Etats, ou (b) par délibération ou application du principe 'ne bis in idem' international. Etant donné que la première option ne peut être soutenue dans un espace européenne de liberté, de sécurité et de justice et ne doit donc pas être recommandée, nous concentrerons nos analyses sur les solutions à l'amiable des conflits, par délibération et dans le respect du principe 'ne bis in idem'.

Plusieurs initiatives visant à introduire le principe international 'ne bis in idem' ont été entreprises par différentes institutions, certaines plus réussies que d'autres. Une étude de ces traités montre que ce principe est largement reconnu au niveau européen. Même si le principe 'ne bis in idem' universel n'est pas encore accepté de façon générale, il est clair qu'un progrès important a déjà été fait.

Toutefois, l'existence de plusieurs lacunes dans le principe 'ne bis in idem' international ont engendré des problèmes juridictionnels supplémentaires. La critique la plus substantielle du principe 'ne bis' existant est son application étriquée au sein de l'acquis de l'UE. Le paragraphe 54 de la Convention de Schengen n'est pertinent que pour les décisions finales, bien qu'il semble plus approprié d'étendre le concept à d'autres décisions, comme par exemple la décision de ne pas poursuivre, la décision de fournir une immunité de poursuites, le règlement alternative et la décision de relaxe.

L'idée d'un principe 'ne bis in idem' plus vaste devrait être en corrélation avec une coopération judiciaire en matière pénale, étant donné que le principe 'ne bis' ne constitue actuellement aucunement les fondements d'un refus de coopération judiciaire en matière pénale. Il est contradictoire d'interdire une deuxième poursuite pour des faits ayant déjà été jugés, mais d'autoriser une coopération judiciaire en matière pénale, telle que l'extradition dans le chef du prévenu. Afin d'éviter que la collaboration entre Etats ne mène à une infraction de ce principe, la coopération judiciaire en matière pénale doit être placée au même niveau que les décisions.

Cela va de pair avec l'absence regrettable d'une banque de données criminelle européenne, puisqu' il est pratiquement impossible à l'heure actuelle pour un Etat d'être informé du fait qu'il y a eu une décision concernant un cas précis dans un autre Etat.

Une seconde option pour la résolution des conflits concrets de compétence serait de restreindre l'application de la compétence par *délibération*. Cette limitation peut être établie de deux façons différentes, qui devraient reposer sur la bonne administration de la justice.

Il est important de souligner que le concept d' une bonne administration de la justice n'implique pas nécessairement une justice rapide et efficace. Il faut aboutir à un certain équilibre entre la nécessité de la poursuite et les considérations d'ordre humanitaire, comme la resocialisation du prévenu, les poursuites dans un pays dont la loi et la langue sont connues du prévenu, les intérêts de la victime, etc. La bonne administration comporte également des considérations concernant les procédures pénales (prévention de poursuites doubles, éviter les condamnations 'in absentia').

La première possibilité est d'établir une hiérarchie dans les critères de compétence, de sorte qu'il soit possible de décider, en vertu d'un traité, quel est l'Etat le plus capable d'entamer des poursuites. Cependant, les efforts visant à dresser une liste des critères n'ont pas véritablement porté leurs fruits car une telle solution hiérarchique semblait trop inflexible et trop mécanique pour convenir à toute situation concrète. Une liste de critères est par conséquent toujours considérée comme irréalisable et indésirable.

La deuxième possibilité, préconisée par le présent article, part de l'idée qu'il est impossible de structurer ces réclamations de façon hiérarchique parce que la décision doit être examinée au cas par cas. Une solution alternative est proposée, partant d'une analyse des critères applicables et sur lesquels un jugement devrait reposer. En outre, il conviendra de veiller à plusieurs exigences organisationnelles nécessaires à la délibération et au contrôle, en opérant une distinction entre les différentes étapes des procédures : la phase de pré-jugement, la phase du jugement et la phase de post-jugement.

Dans le contexte de la délibération, il est important d'attirer l'attention sur le principe de subsidiarité, qui signifie que tous les cas ayant des points de contact dans plus d'un Etat peuvent être délibérés au niveau européen, comme, par exemple, un Belge coupable de vol à l'étalage aux Pays-Bas. Un tel cas tomberait aux mains du ministère public national, et la délibération n'arriverait probablement jamais au niveau international.

En outre, il faut accorder de l'attention à la possibilité de scinder et de fusionner certains cas, spécifiquement dans le cadre d'investigations communes. La question de savoir s'il est préférable de concentrer les incarcérations pour jugement dans un seul Etat membre ou d'assigner plusieurs composants d'un cas complexe à différents pays, avec le problème de savoir quel pays devrait par conséquent être considéré comme compétent pour ces poursuites, devrait avoir une réponse sur la même base que d'autres crimes avec des points de contact dans divers pays.

La délibération peut reposer sur deux types de critères : les critères positifs et les critères négatifs. Les critères positifs de toute sorte sont mentionnés dans plusieurs traités et jugements internationaux. Par exemple, l'article 8 de la Convention Européenne sur la Transmission des Procédures Répressives (1972) indique les cas pour lesquels un Etat contractant peut demander la reprise des procédures par un autre Etat contractant, ce qui est utilisé dans plusieurs autres conventions :

> *'a. si le prévenu a sa résidence habituelle dans l'Etat requis;*
> *b. si le prévenu est un ressortissant de l'Etat requis ou si cet Etat est son Etat d'origine;*
> *c. si le prévenu subit ou doit subir dans l'Etat requis une sanction privative de liberté;*
> *d. si le prévenu fait l'objet dans l'Etat requis d'une poursuite pour la même infraction ou pour d'autres infractions;*
> *e. s'il estime que la transmission est justifiée par l'intérêt de la découverte de la vérité et notamment que les éléments de preuve les plus importants se trouvent dans l'Etat requis;*

f. s'il estime que l'exécution dans l'Etat requis d'une éventuelle condamnation est susceptible d'améliorer les possibilités de reclassement social du condamné;

g. s'il estime que la présence du prévenu ne peut pas être assurée à l'audience dans l'Etat requérant alors que sa présence peut être assurée à l'audience dans l'Etat requis;

h. s'il estime qu'il n'est pas en mesure d'exécuter lui-même une éventuelle condamnation, même en ayant recours à l'extradition, et que l'Etat requis est en mesure de le faire.'

Le Corpus Juris a également consacré l'article 26, alinéa 2 à l'attribution de compétence, listant de façon non-hiérarchique :

'a) l'Etat où se trouvent la majeure partie des preuves,
b) l'Etat de résidence ou de nationalité de l'accusé (ou des principaux accusés),
c) l'Etat où l'impact économique de l'infraction est le plus important.'

La Convention Européenne sur la Transmission des Procédures Répressives et le Corpus Juris comprennent tous deux des critères positifs. Il semble moins fructueux de se concentrer sur les critères négatifs. Cela pourrait par exemple être le cas si le critère de la sanction la plus sévère est décisif. L'analyse des critères positifs et négatifs débouche sur la conclusion que les critères traditionnels sont nécessaires pour l'application de la compétence, mais ne suffisent pas. Une exigence supplémentaire, développée précédemment par l'Institut Américain de Droit, pourrait être le caractère raisonnable « *in concreto* » de l'application de la compétence. La compétence basée sur des critères non-permissibles devrait être prohibée dans tous les cas.

Il semble approprié de créer une liste non-hiérarchique des critères potentiellement raisonnables afin d'améliorer la transparence de la législation européenne. Cette liste pourrait contenir le principe de territorialité, l'article 8 de la Convention Européenne sur la transmission des procédures répressives et les critères dédiés aux victimes, comme le séjour ordinaire, la nationalité ou l'origine de la victime ou le territoire sur lequel a eu lieu le crime. L'achèvement des critères négatifs pourrait être laissé aux organisations judiciaires compétentes, à l'aide d'un développement prétorien. Ceux-ci pourraient être utilisés comme directives pour les poursuites, améliorant la transparence par leur caractère public. Une motivation consciencieuse, mentionnant le critère appliqué, semble essentielle, n'importe quel organisme décide de la choix du forum.

Durant la phase de pré-jugement, la délibération est possible au niveau national, par consultation entre les autorités nationales. Plusieurs instruments de l'UE prévoient d'ores et déjà une procédure de consultation au niveau national, comme par exemple la Convention Européenne du 15 mai 1972 sur la transmission des procédures répressives, qui veille au statut juridique des personnes impliquées tout en leur fournissant certaines garanties. Les Etats nordiques possèdent également un mécanisme de consultation basé sur la confiance, et comparable à la procédure de la Convention Européenne sur la transmission des procédures répressives.

Toutefois, une intervention d'un organe européen tel qu'un Procureur Européen ou Eurojust est favorable, car la délibération entre Etats n'est pas institutionnalisée et ne mène pas automatiquement à une solution pouvant être imposée.

Le Corpus Juris, établi pour la protection des intérêts financiers de l'Union Européenne, semble donner un cadre adéquat. Afin de mener des investigations pour ces types de crimes spécifiques, un Procureur Européen a été proposé, et il semble convenir pour décider de l'attribution de compétence.

L'attribution de la compétence à un Etat Membre par le Procureur Européen peut avoir certaines implications au niveau des obligations internationales de l'Etat Membre, étant donné que ces obligations peuvent comporter des accords concernant l'établissement d'une compétence pour certains cas contradictoires à sa décision. Cette décision comporte cependant plusieurs avantages. Tout d'abord, il sera beaucoup plus facile pour d'autres Etats Membres de reconnaître et donc accepter le jugement de l'Etat en question en comparaison avec une situation où leurs propres autorités auraient également été compétentes pour la décision. La course au plus offrant, par l'accusation ou la défense, pourrait être évitée. En outre, il y aurait moins de risques de situations 'ne bis in idem'.

Pour ce qui est de la révision du choix d'un Etat membre pour le jugement par le Procureur Européen, deux options possibles ont été suggérées. La première repose sur la confiance en tous les systèmes juridiques nationaux, et est de le laisser totalement responsable de son choix. Cela peut être au détriment du prévenu si la cour est sélectionnée de façon inéquitable, car le Procureur Européen pourrait dans ce cas avoir le pouvoir discrétionnaire nécessaire. La deuxième option serait de confier la fonction de révision à la double supervision par le juge des libertés et le tribunal national.

L'idée a été lancée de confier le contrôle du Procureur Européen à une chambre préliminaire Européenne au moment de la clôture des investigations préliminaires afin d'éviter tout contrôle a posteriori. Cette chambre préliminaire a été suggérée en raison des nombreux manquements de la proposition originelle. Tout d'abord, le juge des libertés devra souvent se charger d'une partie des procédures s'étant déroulées dans un pays étranger. Par conséquent, l'hypothèse que ce juge doive appliquer une loi étrangère en plus de sa propre loi et du Corpus Juris, est irréelle. Un autre inconvénient est que la course au plus offrant est possible par le Procureur Européen au cas ou plusieurs juges des libertés sont pris.

Cette chambre pourrait être composée de juges de la Cour de Justice Européenne ou pourrait être un organe totalement neuf, recevant les questions préjudiciables de la part du juge national des libertés. Que les questions soient soulevées par le Procureur Européen ou un citoyen n'est pas clair. Bien que l'option d'une chambre préliminaire semble faisable, elle n'est plus mentionnée dans le Livre Vert.

La proposition visant à donner au Procureur Européen le pouvoir de décider de l'attribution de compétence présente l'avantage théorique de résoudre les problèmes, car la décision du Procureur Européen peut être imposée. Cependant, il semble y avoir davantage d'inconvénients. Tout d'abord, le projet de Corpus Juris est relativement immature, car basé sur un territoire Européen fictif. Ensuite, il n'est établi que pour la protection des intérêts financiers de l'Union Européenne. Et enfin, le Corpus Juris fonctionne du haut vers le bas, et intervient trop fortement dans le pouvoir d'injonction positive des Etats membres.

Une deuxième option est de laisser Eurojust intervenir durant la phase de pré-jugement. Eurojust se compose de procureurs, de magistrats nationaux, ou d'officiers de police de compétence équivalente, détachés par chaque Etat Membre. Au Conseil Européen de Tampere, il fut décidé de créer cet organe afin de faciliter la coordination adéquate des autorités judiciaires nationales via une structure centrale. Cela comprend la tâche de garantir un certain équilibre entre la collaboration policière et judiciaire dans le cadre de l'Union Européenne.

Afin d'atteindre ses objectifs aussi efficacement que possible, Eurojust peut agir par le biais de ses membres nationaux ou en tant que collège. Lorsqu'Eurojust agit par le biais de ses membres nationaux, il peut demander aux autorités compétentes des Etats Membres (I) d'entreprendre des investigations ou d'entamer des poursuites à l'encontre de certains actes, (II) d'accepter qu'un autre Etat membre soit en meilleure position pour entreprendre des investigations, (III) de poursuivre des actes spécifiques et (IV), d'assurer la coordination des autorités compétentes des Etats Membres concernés. En outre, il peut demander (V) la création d'enquête ou de fournir à cette équipe les informations nécessaires pour mener à bien sa tâche. Les compétences d'Eurojust en tant que collège sont approximativement identiques.

Il est crucial de rassembler des informations pour toute décision prise par Eurojust. Par conséquent, la collaboration avec Europol est nécessaire, et ce afin de contribuer à la réalisation d'un espace de liberté, de sécurité et de justice.

Eurojust est seul compétent pour se charger de formes sérieuses de criminalité internationale. Cela comprend les crimes pour lesquels Europol est de tout temps compétent et les crimes tels que la criminalité informatique, la fraude et la corruption ainsi que tout crime touchant aux intérêts financiers de l'Union Européenne, le blanchiment d'argent, les crimes environnementaux et la participation à une organisation criminelle. Conséquence de cette limitation, les Etats l'utilisation des instruments légaux ou des procédures de consultation (transmission des procédures) reste nécessaire.

Eurojust présente l'avantage de fonctionner du bas vers le haut, et de pouvoir demander aux autorités compétentes des Etats Membres d'accepter qu'un autre Etat Membre soit mieux à même de lancer des poursuites. Cette recommandation possède une valeur, car Eurojust possède une grande autorité dans la pratique mais cela n'altère pas le fait qu'il n'a pas la compétence de décider en autorité judiciaire quel Etat est le mieux à même de lancer des poursuites lorsqu'il y a un conflit de compétence. Une décision d'Eurojust ne peut pas, en d'autres termes, être imposée avec le mandat existant. Une solution serait de donner à Eurojust le pouvoir de demander une question préliminaire à la Cour de Justice Européenne sur la question de savoir si leur décision d'une certaine attribution n'est pas déraisonnable. Ce test marginal devrait être non-contraignant. Bien qu'il semble que le mandat d'Eurojust soit suffisamment fort, certains pensent qu'Eurojust devrait avoir un rôle décisionnel dans les affaires judiciaires.

La deuxième étape des procédures à laquelle on peut attribuer les crimes est la phase de jugement. A l'heure actuelle, la plupart des crimes liés à plusieurs pays sont pris en charge au niveau national, par les autorités nationales. Etant donné que le juge national est compétent pour terminer la dernière étape des poursuites, il devrait être la personne apte à déterminer s'il est fondé que son pays soit autorisé à traiter le cas, et sa décision ne devrait pas reposer sur une compétence appliquée de façon déraisonnable. Il devrait toujours vérifier que la décision de l'attribution des poursuites n'affecte pas le statut juridique des personnes concernées. Un juge national n'est pas obligé de suivre les choix faits dans la phase de pré-jugement, même lorsqu'une instance Européenne est intervenue. Il peut se déclarer incompétent lorsqu'il pense que la compétence appliquée par son pays ne repose pas sur une compétence appliquée de façon raisonnable.

Néanmoins, une extension des compétences de la Cour de Justice Européenne (article 35 du Traité d'Amsterdam) visant à donner des jugements préliminaires sur des affaires juridictionnelles vaudrait la peine d'être prise en considération. L'idée est de rendre un juge national d'un des Etats Membres de l'UE compétent pour demander à la Cour de Justice de donner un jugement préliminaire non-contraignant sur la question de savoir si son pays est le mieux à même de lancer des poursuites, à moins qu'Eurojust ait déjà posé une telle question.

En troisième lieu, la phase de post-jugement fournit des opportunités de revoir la décision de savoir quel est le pays compétent pour les poursuites. Etant donné que cette décision influence le statut juridique des victimes et des prévenus, on peut discuter sur le fait qu'une compétence appliquée de façon déraisonnable constitue une infraction à l'article 6 de la Convention Européenne des Droits de l'Homme. La Cour Européenne des Droits de l'Homme pourrait par conséquent condamner un Etat à la demande d'une des parties pour non-respect des règles de jugement équitable et d'application de compétence sur base arbitraire.

La Cour Internationale de Justice a également un rôle a jouer pendant la phase de post-jugement. Cette cour possède une compétence pour tous les cas auxquels se réfèrent les parties et concernant tous les domaines prévus par la Charte des Nations Unies ou les traités et convention en vigueur. La pertinence pour la recherche est qu'un Etat peut demander à la Cour Internationale de Justice de vérifier que la compétence appliquée est ou non contraire à la législation internationale.

Une troisième proposition pendant la phase de post-jugement est de créer une procédure d'appel à la Cour Européenne de Justice. Le Corpus Juris prévoit dans l'article 28 que la Cour Européenne de Justice possède la compétence pour juger les crimes perpétrés à l'encontre des intérêts financiers de l'UE. Cela signifie qu'un appel est possible sur demande du Procureur Européen ou d'une autorité légale nationale pour des conflits de compétence concernant l'application des règles du principe de territorialité européenne, ou la demande du Procureur Européen dans l'exercice du contrôle judiciaire par les tribunaux nationaux. Cela comprend également la compétence de faire passer un jugement sur le choix de forum sur demande de l'accusé.

L'idée d'appel à la Cour de Justice au cours de la phase de post-jugement pourrait être étendue à d'autres crimes. Toutefois, un changement dans le traité serait nécessaire si la Cour de Justice devait être rendue compétente pour les crimes commis à l'encontre des intérêts financiers de l'UE ou pour des crimes plus variés. Cela ne semble pas faisable au vu du temps que prennent les nations pour la ratification.

En conclusion, une convention détaillée est recommandée, comprenant tout d'abord la recommandation pour les Etats Membres de réduire leurs établissement de compétence législative et ensuite de ne recommander et de n'appliquer que sur base de réclamations raisonnables. Une liste non-hiérachique des critères potentiellement raisonnables, comprenant le principe de territorialité, l'article 8 de la Convention Européenne de transmission des procédures répressives et les critères dédiés aux victimes, semble être une solution appropriée pour améliorer la transparence de la législation européenne. Une motivation sérieuse de toute décision concernant l'attribution de compétence pourrait promouvoir cette transparence. En outre, il conviendrait de donner au principe ne bis in idem existant dans cette convention un nouveau contenu plus vaste. Enfin, il est important que cette convention protège le statut et les intérêts légaux du prévenu et de la victime.

Part VII. Recommandation : Projet de convention sur la prévention et la solution des conflits de compétence

Préface

Les Etats membres de l'Union Européenne, dénommés ci-après « les Etats Membres »,

Au vu des étroites relations qui unissent les nations,

Déterminées à collaborer dans leur lutte contre la criminalité dépassant de plus en plus les frontières des Etats,

Etant d'avis que, en ce sens, il serait utile de conclure, dans un esprit de confiance mutuelle, un accord au niveau de l'Union Européenne pour poursuivre en justice les actes criminels,

Exprimant par là-même la confiance dans la structure et dans le fonctionnement des systèmes judiciaires de chaque Etat et dans la capacité de tous les Etats Membres de garantir un jugement équitable,

Guidées par le souhait d'élargir la collaboration dans les affaires criminelles sur base d'une confiance mutuelle, du respect et de la compréhension,

Considérant que :

(1) L'article 31, d du Traité de l'Union Européenne stipule que l'action commune au niveau de la collaboration judiciaire comprend la prévention des conflits de compétence entre les Etats Membres ;

(2) Le numéro 49 e) du plan d'action du 3 décembre 1998 du Conseil et de la Commission concernant les modalités optimales de mise en oeuvre des dispositions du Traité d'Amsterdam relatives à l'établissement d'un espace de liberté, de sécurité et de justice, recommande la mise en place de mesures visant à la coordination des investigations et des poursuites judiciaires dans les Etats Membres, afin d'éviter des jugements doubles et contradictoires, et en tenant compte de la meilleure application du principe ne bis in idem ;

(3) La décision du Conseil en date du 28 février 2002, établissant Eurojust en vue de renforcer la lutte contre la criminalité, et plus spécifiquement l'article 3, qui décrit sa mission comme étant de stimuler et d'améliorer la coordination des investigations et des poursuites au sein des Etats Membres, d'améliorer la collaboration entre les autorités compétentes des Etats Membres et de soutenir les autorités compétentes des Etats Membres afin de rendre leurs investigations

et leurs poursuites plus efficaces, ainsi que les articles 6 et 7, définissant les tâches d'Eurojust, fonctionnant via ses membres nationaux et comme Collège ;

SONT CONVENUES CE QUI SUIT:

Titre I
Dispositions générales

Article premier
Relations avec les autres instruments juridiques

L' objectif de la présente Convention est de compléter les dispositions de toutes les conventions et autres instruments juridiques existants entre les Etats Membres et concernant la collaboration juridique dans les affaires criminelles, et de faciliter leur application entre les Etats Membres.

Article 2
Dispositions liées à l'acquis de Schengen

1. Les dispositions des articles 5 jusque 8 constituent des mesures modifiant ou s'appuyant sur les dispositions visées à l'annexe A de l'accord conclu par le Conseil de l'Union européenne, la République d'Islande et le Royaume de Norvège sur l'association de ces deux États à la mise en oeuvre, à l'application et au développement de l'acquis de Schengen.
2. Les dispositions des articles 54 jusque 58 de la convention d'application Schengen sont abrogées.

Article 3
Définitions

Aux fins de la présente Convention :

a) « la compétence législative » signifiera la compétence d'un Etat Membre à déterminer la portée de son droit pénal, couvrant le droit d'un Etat Membre de considérer certains faits comme étant des actes criminels et d'élaborer des dispositions de droit pénal permettant de sanctionner les infractions de ces actes.
b) « la compétence juridictionelle » signifiera la compétence exécutive permettant de poursuivre des actes sur base des dispositions susmentionnées afin de sanctionner ces actes.

Titre II
Compétence législative

Article 4
Compétence extraterritoriale et territoriale

Chaque Etat Membre évitera les conflits de compétence en limitant la portée de sa compétence extraterritoriale, à moins que des instruments juridiques internationaux la définissent autrement. En outre, le concept de territorialité ne sera pas interprété de sorte que les faits produisant seulement un effet sur le territoire soient considérés comme commis sur le territoire.

Titre III
Compétence juridictionelle

Chapitre premier
Ne bis in idem

Article 5
Sentence finale

Une personne qui a fait l'objet d'un jugement répressif européen ne peut, pour le même fait, être poursuivie dans un autre Etat contractant :
a)   lorsqu'elle a été acquittée
b)   lorsque la sanction infligée :
    1.   a été entièrement subie ou est en cours d'exécution, ou
    2.   a fait l'objet d'une grâce ou d'une amnistie portant sur la totalité de la sanction ou sur la partie non exécutée de celle-ci, ou
    3.   ne peut plus être exécutée en raison de la prescription
c)   lorsque le juge a constaté la culpabilité de l'auteur de l'infraction sans prononcer de sanction.

Article 6
Règlement irrévocable

Personne ne peut être poursuivi dans un Etat Membre pour un fait ayant été réglé irrévocablement dans un autre Etat Membre relativement à cette personne, en satisfaisant une condition spécifique imposée par les autorités compétentes de ce dernier Etat Membre, évitant toute poursuite.

Article 7
Information

1. Lorsqu'une personne est accusée d'une infraction dans un Etat Membre et que les autorités compétentes de cet Etat Membre ont des raisons de croire que

l'accusation concerne les mêmes faits que ceux pour lesquels elle a déjà été définitivement jugée ou que ces faits ont été réglés irrévocablement en satisfaisant une certaine condition dans un autre Etat Membre, ces autorités demanderont, si elles l'estiment nécessaire, les renseignements pertinents aux autorités compétentes de l'Etat Membre concerné ou aux organismes créés conformément à la Traité sur l'Union Européenne.

2. Les informations demandées seront données aussitôt que possible et seront prises en considération pour la suite à réserver à la procédure en cours.

3. Chaque Etat Membre désignera, au moment de la signature, de la ratification, de l'acceptation ou de l'approbation de la présente convention, les autorités qui seront habilitées à demander et à recevoir les informations prévues au présent article.

Article 8
Dispositions nationales plus larges

Les dispositions précédentes ne font pas obstacle à l'application de dispositions nationales plus larges concernant l'effet "ne bis in idem" attaché aux décisions judiciaires prises à l'étranger.

Chapitre 2
Bonne administration de la justice

Article 9
Application déraisonnable de la compétence

Afin d'aboutir à une bonne administration de la justice, les Etats Membres n'appliqueront pas leur compétence lorsque cela serait déraisonnable. L'application de la compétence par un Etat Membre est manifestement déraisonnable si ce n'est pas l'Etat Membre :

1. où le crime a été commis,
2. où la personne suspectée est résidente ordinaire,
3. de la nationalité ou de l'origine de la personne suspectée,
4. où la personne suspectée subit ou va subir un jugement impliquant la privation de liberté,
5. où des procédures pour le même ou d'autres crimes sont en œuvre à l'encontre de la personne suspectée, par les autorités judiciaires,
6. où les preuves les plus importantes sont situées,
7. où l'application d'un jugement futur est susceptible d'améliorer les perspectives de réhabilitation sociale du prévenu,
8. où la présence aux audiences de la personne suspectée peut être garantie,
9. où un éventuel jugement peut être appliqué,
10. où la victime est résidente ordinaire,
11. de la nationalité ou de l'origine de la victime ou,
12. où le dommage se présente.

Article 10
Autorités nationales

Si plusieurs Etats Membres possèdent la compétence pour certains actes et ce sans préjudice aucun aux articles 30 et 33 de la Convention Européenne du 15 mai 1972 sur la transmission des procédures répressives, les autorités judiciaires compétentes de chaque Etat Membre collaboreront afin de s'accorder sur le ou les Etats Membres étant dans une position raisonnable que pour appliquer la compétence .

Article 11
Eurojust

Lorsqu'elle accomplit ses tâches, recommandées par l'article 6 de la Décision du Conseil du 28 février 2002 instituant Eurojust afin de renforcer la lutte contre les formes graves de criminalité, Eurojust favorisera l'application raisonnable de la compétence juridictionelle.

Article 12
Juge national

Tout tribunal ou cour d'un Etat Membre peut demander à la Cour Européenne de Justice d'émettre un jugement préliminaire sur une question soulevée dans une affaire en suspens afin de savoir si l'application de la compétence juridictionelle par son pays est déraisonnable si cette cour ou ce tribunal considère qu'une décision sur la question est nécessaire pour lui permettre d'émettre son jugement.

Titre IV
La coopération judiciaire en matière pénale

Article 13

1. Un Etat Membre ne donnera pas suite à une demande de coopération judiciaire en matière pénale émanant d'un autre Etat Membre si la procédure étant à l'origine de la demande concerne une personne acquittée dans un Etat Membre pour les mêmes faits punissables que ceux relatifs à la demande, ou encore qui, en cas de jugement, si aucune sanction n'a été prononcée, si la personne a déjà subi la sanction ou la subit encore ou si selon la loi de cet Etat Membre la personne ne peut plus être soumise à l'exécution de la sanction parce qu'elle a été graciée, amnistiée ou parce qu'il y a prescription.
2. Un Etat Membre ne donnera pas suite à une demande de coopération judiciaire en matière pénale émanant d'un autre Etat Membre si les faits relatifs à la demande ont déjà été réglés irrevocablement dans un Etat Membre, à la satisfaction d'une condition.
3. Un Etat Membre peut refuser de donner suite à une demande de coopération judiciaire en matière pénale émanant d'un autre Etat Membre si la procédure

étant à l'origine de la demande concerne une personne acquittée dans un Etat tiers pour les mêmes faits punissables que ceux relatifs à la demande, ou encore qui, en cas de jugement, si aucune sanction n'a été prononcée, si la personne a déjà subi la sanction ou la subit encore ou si selon la loi de cet Etat Membre la personne ne peut plus être soumise à l'exécution de la sanction parce qu'elle a été graciée, amnistiée ou parce qu'il y a prescription.

4. Un Etat Membre ne donnera pas suite à une demande coopération judiciaire en matière pénale émanant d'un autre Etat Membre si les faits relatifs à la demande ont déjà été réglés irrévocablement dans un Etat tiers, à la satisfaction d'une condition.

5. Cet article élargit les bases de refus de demande de coopération judiciaire en matière pénale, telle que recommandée dans les conventions existantes.

Titre V
Dispositions finales

Article 14
Réserves

La présente convention ne peut faire l'objet d'aucune réserve.

Article 15
Application territoriale

La présente convention s'appliquera à Gibraltar.

Article 16
Entrée en vigueur

1. La présente convention est soumise à adoption par les États Membres conformément à leurs règles constitutionnelles respectives.

2. Les États Membres notifient au secrétaire général du Conseil de l'Union européenne l'accomplissement des procédures requises par leurs règles constitutionnelles pour l'adoption de la présente convention.

3. La présente convention entre en vigueur quatre-vingt-dix jours après la notification visée au paragraphe 2, par l'État, membre de l'Union européenne au moment de l'adoption par le Conseil de l'acte établissant la présente convention, qui procède le huitième à cette formalité, dans les huit États Membres concernés.

4. Toute notification faite par un État Membre postérieurement à la réception de la huitième notification visée au paragraphe 2 a pour effet que, quatre-vingt-dix jours après cette notification postérieure, la présente convention entre en vigueur entre cet État Membre et les États Membres pour lesquels la convention est déjà entrée en vigueur.

5. Avant l'entrée en vigueur de la convention en vertu du paragraphe 3, chaque État Membre peut, lorsqu'il procède à la notification visée au paragraphe 2 ou à tout moment après cette notification, déclarer que la présente convention est

applicable dans ses rapports avec les États Membres qui ont fait la même déclaration. Ces déclarations prennent effet quatre-vingt-dix jours après la date de leur dépôt.

6. La présente convention s'applique à des faits pour lesquels aucune décision finale n'a été prise après la date à laquelle elle est entrée en vigueur, ou est appliquée en vertu du paragraphe 5, entre les États Membres concernés.

Article 17
Adhésion de nouveaux États Membres

1. La présente convention est ouverte à l'adhésion de tout État qui devient membre de l'Union européenne.

2. Le texte de la présente convention dans la langue de l'État adhérent, établi par le Conseil de l'Union européenne, fait foi.

3. Les instruments d'adhésion sont déposés auprès du dépositaire.

4. La présente convention entre en vigueur à l'égard de tout État qui y adhère quatre-vingt-dix jours après le dépôt de son instrument d'adhésion, ou à la date de son entrée en vigueur si elle n'est pas encore entrée en vigueur au moment de l'expiration de ladite période de quatre-vingt-dix jours.

5. Si la présente convention n'est pas encore entrée en vigueur lors du dépôt de leur instrument d'adhésion, l'article 16, paragraphe 5, s'applique aux États adhérents.

Article 18
Entrée en vigueur pour l'Islande et la Norvège

1. Sans préjudice de l'article 8 de l'accord conclu par le Conseil de l'Union européenne avec la République d'Islande et le Royaume de Norvège concernant l'association de ces États à la mise en œuvre, à l'application et au développement de l'acquis de Schengen ("l'accord d'association"), les dispositions visées à l'article 2, paragraphe 1, entrent en vigueur pour l'Islande et la Norvège quatre-vingt-dix jours après réception, par le Conseil et la Commission, des informations prévues à l'article 8, paragraphe 2, de l'accord d'association concernant la satisfaction de leurs exigences constitutionnelles, dans leurs relations respectives avec tout État Membre pour lequel cette convention est déjà entrée en vigueur en vertu de l'article 27, paragraphe 3 ou 4.

2. Toute entrée en vigueur de la présente convention pour un État Membre après la date d'entrée en vigueur des dispositions visées à l'article 2, paragraphe 1, pour l'Islande et la Norvège, rend ces dispositions également applicables dans les relations entre cet État Membre et l'Islande et entre cet État Membre et la Norvège.

3. En tout état de cause, les dispositions visées à l'article 2, paragraphe 1, ne lient pas l'Islande et la Norvège avant la date qui sera fixée conformément à l'article 15, paragraphe 4, de l'accord d'association.

4. Sans préjudice des paragraphes 1, 2 et 3, l'entrée en vigueur des dispositions visées à l'article 2, paragraphe 1, pour l'Islande et la Norvège a lieu au plus tard à

la date d'entrée en vigueur de la présente convention pour le quinzième État, membre de l'Union européenne au moment de l'adoption par le Conseil de l'acte établissant la présente convention.

Article 19
Dépositaire

1. Le secrétaire général du Conseil de l'Union européenne est dépositaire de la présente convention.
2. Le dépositaire publie au Journal officiel des Communautés européennes l'état des adoptions et des adhésions, les déclarations et les réserves, ainsi que toute autre notification relative à la présente convention.

Bibliography

Section 1. Literature

ANCEL, M., *La défence sociale nouvelle. Un mouvement de politique criminelle humaniste*, Parijs, Cujas, 1954, 183 p.

ANCEL, M., *La défence sociale*, Parijs, Presses Universitaires de France, 1989, 127 p.

BAAIJENS-VAN GELOVEN, Y.G.M., *Overdracht en overname van strafvervolging*, Arnhem, Gouda Quint, 1996, 473 p.

BASSIOUNI, M.C., *A draft international criminal code and draft statute for an international criminal tribunal*, Dordrecht, Boston, Lancaster, Martinus Nijhoff Publishers, 1987, 492 p.

BERTHELET P. and CHEVALLIER-GOVERS, C., Quelle relation entre Europol et Eurojust? Rapport d'égalité ou rapport d'autorité?, *Revue du Marché commun et de l'Union européenne*, n°450, juillet-août 2001, 468-474.

BEULKE, W. , *Strafprozessrecht*, Heidelberg, C.F. Müller Verlag, 2000, 224-225.

BOS M., 'The extraterritorial jurisdiction of states', *Institute of International Law, Yearbook*, 1993, part I, 13-190.

BROWNLIE, I., *Principles of public international law,* Oxford, Clarendon Press, 1990, 743 p.

CHOO, A. L.-T., *Abuse of process and judicial stays of criminal proceedings*, Oxford, Clarendon Press, 1993, 207 p.

DELMAS-MARTY, M., *Corpus Juris, portant dispositions pénales pour la protection des intérêts financiers de l'Union européenne,* Antwerpen-Groningen-Oxford, Intersentia Rechtswetenschappen, 1998, 189 p.

DELMAS-MARTY, and M.; VERVAELE, J.A.E., The implementation of the Corpus Juris in the Member States, Vol I, Antwerpen-Groningen-Oxford, Intersentia, 2000, 394 p.

DELMAS-MARTY, M. and VERVAELE, J.A.E., *The implementation of the Corpus Juris in the Member States volume IV*, Antwerpen-Groningen-Oxford, Intersentia, 2001, 530 p.

DE RUYVER, B., *De strafrechtelijke politiek gevoerd onder de socialistische Ministers van Justitie, E. Vandervelde, P. Vermeylen en A. Vranckx,* Antwerpen-Arnhem, Kluwer-Gouda Quint, 1988, 182 p.

DE SCHUTTER, B., 'Samenwerking in strafzaken en pogingen tot harmonisatie van het strafrecht in de Beneluxlanden', *Droit pénal européen, Europees Strafrecht, European criminal law,* Brussel, Presses Universitaires de Bruxelles, 1970, 580-593.

DE SCHUTTER, B., 'Problems of jurisdiction in the international control of repression of terrorism', in *International terrorism and political crimes,* M.C. BASSIOUNI (ed.), Springfield, Illinois, Charles Thomas Publisher, 1975, 377-390.

DONNEDIEU DE VARBES, H., *Les principes modernes du droit pénal international,* Sirey, Paris, 1928, 511-536.

ERA, *ERA-forum* 3, Study on 'penal and administrative sanctions, settlement, whistleblowing and Corpus Juris in the candidate countries', 2001.

FAYARD, M.-C.; 'La localisation internationale de l'infraction', *Revue de Science Criminelle et de Droit Pénal Comparé,* 1968, 753-779.

FELLER, S.Z., 'Jurisdiction over offences with a foreign element', in *A treatise on international criminal law,* BASSIOUNI, M.C.; NANDA, V.P. (eds.), Springfield, Illinois, Charles Thomas Publisher, 1973, Vol. II, 5-64.

FELLER, S.Z., Concurrent criminal jurisdiction in the international sphere, *Israel law review,* 1981, 41-74.

HARVARD LAW SCHOOL, 'Jurisdiction with respect to crime. Draft convention, with comment, prepared by the research in international law of the Harvard Law School', *Supplement to the American Journal of International Law,* 1935, 439-651.

HIGGINS, R., *Problems and process. International law and how we use it,* Oxford, Clarendon Press, 1994, 274 p.

INGELSE, C. and VAN DER WILT, H., De zaak Pinochet. Over universele rechtsmacht en Hollandse benepenheid, *NJB* (Ned.) 1996, 280-285.

JENNINGS, R. and WATTS, A., *Oppenheim's international law,* London-New-York, 1996, volume I.Peace, 2 v.

JUSTICE, EU cooperation in criminal matters, response to specific proposals, February 2001, URL: http://www.justice.org.uk/publications/listofpublications/index.html.

LAGODNY, O., 'Empfiehlt es sich, eine europäische Gerichtskompetenz für Strafgewaltskonflikte vorzusehen?', Gutachten im Auftrag des Bundesministeriums der Justiz, Berlin, März, 2001, unpublished, 151 p.

LAMBERT, J.J., *Terrorims and hostages in international law. A commentary on the Hostages Convention 1979, Cambridge,* Grotius Publications, 1990, 418 p.

MANN, F.A., 'The international doctrine of jurisdiction in international law', *Collected Courese of the Hague Academy of International Law*, 1964, 1-162.

MANN, F.A., 'The doctrine of international jurisdiction revisited after twenty years', *Collected Courese of the Hague Academy of International Law*, 1984, 9-116.

MERON, T., 'International criminalization of internal atrocities', *American Journal of International Law*, 1995, 554-577.

MORRISON, F.L., *German Yearbook of international law*, 1986, 417-434.

MOK, M.R. and DIJK, R.A.A., 'Toepassing van het Nederlands strafrecht op buiten Nederland begane delicten', *Handelingen 1980 der Nederlandse Juristen-Vereniging deel 1, tweede stuk*, 1980, 3-149.

MÜLLER-RAPPARD, E. and BASSIOUNI, M.C., European inter-state cooperation in criminal matters, 1991, *E.T.S.* n°73.

OEHLER, D., *Internationales Strafrecht. Geltungsbereich des Strafrechts. Internationales Rechtshilfrecht. Recht der Gemeinschaften, Völkerstrafrecht,* Köln-Berlin-Bonn-München, Carl Heymanns Verlag KG, 1983, 689 p.

ORIE, A.M.M., 'Internationale strafrechtelijke aspecten van de Dost-affaire', *Nederlands Juristenblad*, 1976, 1045-1059.

ORIE, A.M.M., VAN DER MEIJS, J.G. and SMIT, A.M.G., *Internationaal strafrecht*, Zwolle, Tjeenk Willink, 1991, 190 p.

PAUST, J.J., BASSIOUNI, M.C., WILLIAMS, S., SCHARF, M., GURULLÉ J. and ZAGARIS, B., *International Criminal Law. Cases and Materials*, Durham – North Carolina, Carolina Academic Press, 1996, 1438 p.

PAPPAS, C., *Stellvertretende Strafrechtsplege. Zugleich ein Beitrag zur Ausdehnung deutscher Strafgewalt nach § 7 Abs. 2 Nr. 2 StGB*, Freiburg im Breisgau, Max-Planck-Institut für ausländisches und internationales Strafrecht, 1996, 262 p.

ROGALL, K., 'Grundsatzfragen der Beweisverbote' in *Beweisverbote in Ländern der EU und vergleichbaren Rechtsordnungen / Exclusion of Evidence Within the EU and Beyond*, F. HÖPFEL and B. HUBER (eds.), Freiburg im Breisgau, Max-

Planck-Institut für ausländisches und internationals Strafrecht, 1999, 119-148 (139-140).

SCHACHTER, O., *International Law in theory and practice*, Dordrecht – Boston – Londen, Martinus Nijhoff Publishers, 1991, 431 p.

SCREVENS, R., 'Collaboration en matière pénale et tentatives d'harmonisation du droit pénal dans certains groupes d'états', *Droit pénal européen, Europees Strafrecht, European Criminal Law*, Brussel, Presses Universitaires de Bruxelles, 1970, 599-629.

STESSENS, G., 'Het Corpus Juris in een stroomversnelling, het Europees openbaar ministerie in aantocht?', *Panopticon* 2000, 271-276.

STRIJARDS, G.A.M., *Internationaal strafrecht. Strafmachtsrecht*, Arnhem, Gouda Quint, 1984, Algemeen deel, 355 p.

SUNGA, L.S., *The emerging system of international criminal law. Developments of codification and implementation*. Den Haag-London-Boston, Kluwer law International, 1997, 486 p.

SWART, A.H.J., 'De overdracht van strafvervolgingen', *Nederlands Juristenblad*, 1982, 209-223.

SWART, A.H.J., *Goede rechtsbedeling en internationale rechtshulp in strafzaken*, Deventer, Kluwer, 1983, 28 (I).

SWART, A.H.J., 'Internationalisering van de strafrechtspleging', in C. KELK e.a.. (eds.), *Grenzen en mogelijkheden. Opstellen over en rondom de strafrechtspleging*, Nijmegen, Ars Aequi Libri, 1984, 112-129.

THOMAS, F., *De Europese rechtshulpverdragen in strafzaken. Ontstaan en evolutie van een Europees strafrechtsbeleid van uitlevering tot overdracht van strafvervolging,* Gent, Story Scientia, 1980, 536 p.

VAN DEN WYNGAERT, C., *The political offence exception to extradition. The delicate problem of balancing the rights of the individual and the international public order,* Boston-Antwerpen-London-Frankfurt, Kluwer, 1980, 263 p.

VAN DEN WYNGAERT, C., *The transformations of international criminal law as a response to the challenge of organised crime*, Antwerpen, Universitaire Instelling Antwerpen, 1998, 94 p.

VAN DEN WYNGAERT, C., 'Corpus Juris, parquet européen et juge national vers une chambre préliminaire européenne', *Agon,* 1999, N° 23, 2-6.

VANDER BEKEN, T., *Forumverdeling in het internationaal strafrecht. De verdeling van misdrijven met aanknopingspunten in meerdere staten*, Antwerpen-Apeldoorn, Maklu-uitgevers, 1999, 486 p.

VANDER BEKEN, T., 'De moeilijke zoektocht naar het beste forum voor internationale misdrijven. De ad hoc tribunalen als ideale oplossing?', WOUTERS, J. and PANKEN, H. (eds.), *De Genocidewet in internationaal perspectief*, Gent, Larcier, 2002, 75-94.

VAN GERVEN, W., 'Constitutional conditions for a Public Prosecutor's Office at the European level' in DE KERCHOVE, G. and WEYEMBERGH A. (ed.), *Vers un espace judiciaire pénal européen*, Bruxelles, Institut d'études européennes, 2000,373 p.

VERMEULEN, G., VANDER BEKEN T., ZANDERS, P. and DE RUYVER, B., *Internationale samenwerking in strafzaken en rechtsbescherming*, Brussel, Politeia, 1995, 386 p.

VERMEULEN, G., *Wederzijdse rechtshulp in strafzaken in de Europese Unie: naar een volwaardige rechtshulpruimte voor de Lidstaten?*, Antwerpen-Apeldoorn, Maklu, 1999, 632 p.

VERMEULEN, G., VANDER BEKEN, T., DE BUSSER, E., VAN DEN WYNGAERT, C., STESSENS, G., MASSET, A. and MEUNIER, C., *Een nieuwe Belgische wetgeving inzake internationale hulp in strafzaken*, Antwerpen-Apeldoorn, Maklu, 2002, 421 p.

WENGLER, W., 'Völkerrechtliche Schranken der Beeinflussung auslandverknüpften Verhaltens durch Massnahmen des Staatlichen Rechts' in *German Yearbook of International Law*, 1988, 448-477.

WITSCHI, N., *Die Übernahme der Strafverfolgung nach künftigen schweizerischem Recht*, Bern, Verlag Stämpfli, 1977, 136 p.

X., 'Constructing the state extraterritorially: jurisdictional discourse, the national interest and transnational norms', *Harvard Law Review*, 1990,1273-1305.

XANTHAKI, H., *The use of criminal records as a means of preventing organised crime in the areas of money laundering and public procurement: the need for Europe-wide collaboration*, Falcone Project JHA/1999/FAL/197, Sir William Dale Centre for Legislative Studies, London, vol. 1, 99 p.

Section 2. Case Law

PERMANENT COURT OF JUSTICE, The Hague, 7 September 1927, *Revue Internationale de Droit Pénal*, 1927, 326-362.

INTERNATIONAL COURT OF JUSTICE, 5 February 1970, *(Case Concerning the Barcelona Traction, Light and Power Company Limited), International Court of Justice Reports*, 1970.

United States of America v. Cotroni, URL: www2.lexum.umontreal.ca/ca_us/en/cts.1991.37.en.cfm?langue=en.

United States of America v. El Zein, URL: http://www.lexum.umontreal.ca/csc-scc/en/pub/1989/vol1/html/1989scr1_1469.html.

INTERNATIONAL COURT OF JUSTICE, Case concerning the arrest warrant of 11 April 2000, Democratic Republic of the Congo v. Belgium, 14 February 2002, N° 121.

Section 3. Legal Documents

I. European Union

Convention of 25 May 1987 between the Member States of the European Communities on double jeopardy, URL: ue.eu.int/ejn/data/vol_a/accords_ce/CPEIIen.html.

The Convention on the protection of the European Community's financial interests of 26 July 1995, OJ C313, 23/10/1996.

Convention of 26 July 1995 on the establishment of a European police office, OJ C316, 27/11/1995

First Protocol of 27 September 1996, OJ C313, 23/10/1996.

Protocol of 29 November 1996 on the interpretation of the PFI Convention and its Protocols by the Court of Justice, OJ C 151, 20/05/1997.

Second Protocol of 19 June 1997, OJ C 221, 19/07/1997.

Action Plan of 3 December 1998 of the Council and the Commission on how best to implement the provisions of the Treaty of Amsterdam in the areas of freedom, security, and justice, OJ C 19, 23 January 1999, URL: europa.eu.int/scadplus/leg/en/lvb/l33080.htm.

Corpus Juris 2000, Florence, May 1999, *ERA-forum* 3, 2001, p. 53-60.

Tampere European Council of 15 and 16 October 1999, Presidency conclusions, URL://europa.eu.int/council/off/conclu/oct99/oct99_en.htm.

COUNCIL OF THE EUROPEAN UNION, Exploratory thoughts concerning Eurojust, Brussels, 4 February 2000.

Council Framework Decision of 29 May 2000 on increasing protection by criminal penalties and other sanctions against counterfeiting in connection with the introduction of the Euro, *O.J.*, 14.6.2000, L 140.

COUNCIL OF THE EUROPEAN UNION, evaluation report on Finland on Mutual Legal Assistance and Urgent Requests for the Tracing and Restraint of property, Brussels, 7 July 2000, 43 p., URL: ue.eu.int/ejn/data/evaluation/09392.en.pdf.

COMMISSION OF THE EUROPEAN UNION, Communication of the commission to the Council on mutual recognition of final decisions in criminal matters, Brussels 26/07/2000, COM(2000) 495 final.

CONFERENCE OF THE REPRESENTATIVES OF THE GOVERNMENTS OF THE MEMBER STATES, IGC 2000: Incorporation of a reference to Eurojust in the Treaty, Brussels, 19 November 2000.

Charter of Fundamental Rights of the European Union, OJ C 364, 18 December 2000.

Council decision of 14 December 2000 setting up a Provisional Judicial Co-operation Unit, OJ L 324, 21 December 2000.

EUROPEAN COMMISSION, Mutual Recognition of Decisions in Criminal Matters among the EU Member States and Jurisdiction, Discussion Paper with questions for experts, 2001, unpublished.

COMMISSION OF THE EUROPEAN COMMUNITIES, Proposal for a Directive of the European Parliament and of the Council on the criminal-law protection of the Community's financial interests, Brussels, 23/05/2001, COM(2001) 272final.

EUROPEAN PARLIAMENT, Draft opinion on the proposal for a directive on the criminal-law protection of the Community's financial interests, 12/10/2001, 2001/0115(COD).

COUNCIL OF THE EUROPAN UNION, proposal for a Council Framework Decision on combating terrorism, Brussels, 7 December 2001.

COMMISSION OF THE EUROPEAN COMMUNITIES, Green Paper on criminal-law protection of the financial interests of the Community and the establishment of a European Prosecutor, Brussels, 11/12/2001, COM(2001) 715 final, URL: europa.eu.int/comm/anti_fraud/livre_vert.

COMITE DE SURVEILLANCE DE L'OLAF, 'Avis 2/2002 sur le Livre Vert sur la protection pénales des intérêts financiers communautaires et la création du Procureur Européen', *Agon*, N° 34, 2002, 3-8.

Council decision of 28 February 2002 setting up Eurojust with a view to reinforcing the fight against serious crime, OJ L 63, 6 March 2002.

II. Council of Europe

European Convention on extradition, Paris, 13 December 1957, E.T.S., N° 024, URL: conventions.coe.int/treaty/en/treaties/html/024.htm.

European Convention on the international validity of criminal judgments, The Hague, 28 May 1970, E.T.S. N° 70, URL: ue.eu.int/ejn/data/vol_b/4b_convention_protocole_accords/entraide_judic_penal e/070texten.html.

COUNCIL OF EUROPE, EUROPEAN COMMITTEE ON CRIME PROBLEMS, Extraterritorial criminal jurisdiction, Strasbourg, 1990, 26.

III. Others

Treaty on International Penal Law, Montevideo, 23 January 1889, *Supplement to the American Jounal of International Law*, 1935, 638-639.

Statute of the International Court of Justice, 25 June 1945, URL: www.icj-cij.org/icjwww/ibasicdocuments/ibasictext/ibasicstatute.htm.

Agreement between the Parties to the North Atlantic Treaty regarding the status of their forces, London, 19 June 1951 in VERMEULEN, G.; VANDER BEKEN, T., *Compendium Internationaal Strafrecht*, IA, 19/06/51, 1-19, URL: www.nato.int/docu/basictxt/b510619a.htm.

Benelux Convention, Bussels, 26 September 1968, *Trb.* 1969, nr. 9.

Convention 29 avril 1969 concernant la coopération administrative et judiciaire dans le domaine des réglementations se rapportant à la réalisation des objectifs de l'Union économique Benelux, La Haye, *Moniteur Belge*, 17 february 1971.

Protocol amending the Treaty on extradition between the Government of Canada and the Government of the United States of America, Washington, 3 December 1971, URL: www2.lexum.umontreal.ca/ca_us/en/cts.1991.37.en.cfm?langue=en.

Benelux Convention, Brussels, 11 May 1974, *Trb.*, 1974, nr. 184.

Convention of 19 June 1990 applying the Schengen Agreement of 14 June 1985 between the Governments of the States of the Benelux Economic Union, the

Federal Republic of Germany and the French Republic, on the gradual abolition of checks at their common borders, URL: ue.eu.int/ejn/data/vol_c/9_autres_textes/schengen/indexen.html.

Rome Statute of the International Criminal Court, 17 July 1998, URL, www.un.org/law/icc/statute/romefra.htm.